What Did It Say First?

Hearing the Bibles In It's Own Words

Rene' Stanley

Books by Rene'

ISBN: 979-8-9997823-8-0

Library of Congress Control Number: 2026907041

Book Cover by Rene' Stanley

First edition 2026

Https://bbr.booksbyrene.com

Contents

Part V

Time, Judgement, Law, and "Hell"

ACKNOWLEDGEMENTS

To everyone who helped me hear the Bible "again," I owe more than I can say.

I am grateful for the scholars, pastors, and teachers whose careful work in Hebrew, Greek, and the history of the canon underlies every chapter here. Any mistakes are mine alone, but whatever is accurate and helpful has been shaped by generations of men and women who loved both the church and the text. Their articles, commentaries, gave me the confidence to speak simply without being careless.

I also want to thank the communities across Christian traditions—Protestant, Catholic, and Orthodox—who reminded me that the Bible has never belonged to just one group. Conversations with believers from different canons and cultures opened my eyes to how much we can learn from one another when we listen first and argue second.

Finally, I am grateful to the God whose name and character this book tries, in a very small way, to honor. Every attempt to ask, "What did it say first?" is really an attempt to listen more carefully to Him. May anything true and helpful in these pages lead you closer to the One who still speaks.

This book is meant to be a **toolbox**, not a textbook you must master. You can read it straight through, but it also works well if you dip into the chapters that match what you are wrestling with right now.

1. Start where your questions are

- If you wonder about **God's names** ("LORD," "God," "Jesus," "Christ"), begin with **Part II**.

- If you are unsure what the Bible means by **"soul," "flesh," or "heart,"** try **Part III**.

- If you want clarity on **sin, salvation, grace, faith, righteousness, peace**, go to **Part IV**.

- If your questions are about **hell, judgment, law, covenant, nations**, look at **Part V**.

You don't have to follow the order. Use the Table of Contents like a map and choose a path that fits your current needs.

2. Read with a Bible open

Keep your regular Bible beside you (or open in an app).

For each chapter:

1. Read the **short intro** and look at the **word box** for the key terms.

2. Read the chapter, pausing when a passage is cited to **actually look it up**.

3. At the end, pick one of that chapter's passages and read it again, slowly, with the new word in mind.

The goal is not just to understand the word but to **hear Scripture itself more clearly**.

3. Use the tracks as "mini-courses"

The Parts are arranged as three main "tracks" plus some framing material:

- **Part II** – The Name and Face of God

- **Part III** – What Is a Human Being?

- **Part IV** – Sin, Salvation, and the Good News

- **Part V** – Time, Judgment, Law, and "Hell"

You can treat each track as a short course:

- Read the Part introduction.

- Work through its chapters over a few weeks.

- Jot down one or two "this changes how I read..." notes at the end of each chapter.

Later, you can loop back and take a different track.

4. Keep advanced tools optional

Chapter 31 introduces practical tools (concordances, apps, interlinear features), but you **do not need** to use them for every passage.

A healthy rhythm:

- Most days: simply read a chapter of Scripture and pray.

- Sometimes: when a word stands out, use the tools from Chapter 31 to dig a little deeper.

- Occasionally: follow one key word across a few passages, using the word index and glossary.

Let curiosity lead you rather than guilt. These tools are there when you want them; they're not homework.

5. Reading in groups

If you use this book with others:

- Choose one track or a short cluster of chapters (for example, 11–13 on soul/spirit/body).

- Before each meeting, everyone reads the chapter and one or two of the suggested passages.

- In the group, focus on questions like:

- "What did this word mean first?"

- "How does that change how we hear this passage?"

- "What difference could this make in how we live or pray?"

You don't have to agree on every detail. The point is to **listen together** and let Scripture shape you as a community.

6. When you feel overwhelmed

At any point, if you start to feel buried in terms:

- Step back to something simple: a psalm, a parable, a section of a Gospel.

- Read it in your own language with no tools.

- Then, if you like, notice just **one** word and recall what you've learned about it.

You are not trying to carry every Hebrew and Greek term in your head. You are gradually training your ears so that, more and more, the Bible's own way of speaking can guide how you understand and follow it.

This book is for **ordinary Bible readers** who sense that there is more going on under their English translation and want help hearing it without going to seminary.

- It is for people who **love Scripture** but sometimes feel confused: Why does "soul" sound so ghost-like? Does "law" always mean the same thing? What exactly is "hell" in the Bible's own words?

- It is for those who have heard bits of **Hebrew and Greek**—maybe in sermons or footnotes—and would like a clear, gentle guide that explains what matters without drowning them in grammar.

- It is for **small-group leaders**, Sunday school teachers, and pastors who want simple, reliable ways to explain key terms to others without relying on shaky word tricks or internet rabbit holes.

- It is for readers who are **curious about different canons** (Protestant, Catholic, Orthodox, Ethiopian) and want to know what difference, if any, those lists of books make for how we hear the Bible.

- It is also for those who carry **questions or doubts**: about judgment, hell, salvation, or God's character, and suspect that part of their struggle comes from flattened or fuzzy translations.

This book is **not** only for experts. You do not need to know any Hebrew or Greek to benefit. If you can read an ordinary Bible and are willing to slow down, look carefully, and learn a few new terms along the way, this book is for you.

This book spends a lot of time looking under our English translations—at Hebrew and Greek words, at different canons, at places where meanings get "flattened." It is important to say clearly: **you can still trust your English Bible.** That's why this book exists at all.

1. The main story comes through clearly

Across careful modern translations, the **big story and central message** are the same:

- Who God is: Creator, holy and merciful, slow to anger, rich in love.

- Who we are: made in His image, broken by sin, invited into covenant relationship.

- What God has done in Christ: His life, death, and resurrection for our salvation.

- What He calls us to: repentance, faith, love of God and neighbor, hope in new creation.

No matter which solid translation you use, these things do not change. Small differences in wording do not erase the **core truths** the Bible is giving us.

2. Translations are careful, not casual

Modern Bible translations are:

- Based on **thousands of ancient manuscripts**, carefully compared and studied.

- Produced by **teams of trained scholars** who check each other's work.

- Reviewed and revised over time as we learn more about language and history.

Translators know they are handling something precious. They work slowly, argue about wording, and aim to be **transparent and faithful**, not clever or original. You may prefer one translation's style over another, but most major versions are **trustworthy**.

3. No translation is perfect—and that's okay

Every translation makes **choices**:

- Some aim to stay as close as possible to the original wording ("literal" or "formal" translations).

- Others focus more on clear, natural English ("dynamic" or "thought-for-thought" translations).

This means:

- No English Bible can carry every nuance of every word.

- Sometimes a single English term has to cover several related Hebrew or Greek ideas.

- Occasionally, translations differ in ways that matter for how we hear a verse.

That is why this book talks about **"flattening"** and word ranges. But these limitations do not make translations useless; they simply remind us to be **humble and thoughtful** when we press fine details too hard.

4. Word work is a supplement, not a replacement

The aim of looking at Hebrew and Greek is not to make you **suspicious** of your Bible. It is to:

- Help you notice where a word in English might be doing **double duty**.

- Clarify passages that have always felt confusing or harsh.

- Deepen your confidence that there is usually a **good reason** for the translation in front of you, even if you don't see it at first.

Your English Bible remains your **main text**. Word studies and canon comparisons are tools you take out when needed, not new scriptures that replace the one you already have.

5. God works through real, imperfect translations

Finally, we trust our Bibles not only because of manuscripts and scholarship, but because of **who God is**.

- The God who spoke through prophets and apostles is **not powerless** to make Himself known through translation.

- For centuries, people have met Christ, been changed, and walked faithfully with God using translations far less precise than the ones you hold today.

- When you come to Scripture with a willing heart, God is able to **guide, correct, and teach you**, even when wording is less than ideal.

This book invites you to listen more carefully, not to live in fear of getting everything wrong. Your English Bible is a **gift**, and it is more than sufficient to lead you to the God it speaks of. Learning what lies beneath its words is simply a way of saying "thank you" with your mind as well as your heart.

How To Use This Book

This book is meant to be a toolbox, not a textbook you must master. You can read it straight through, but it also works well if you dip into the chapters that match what you are wrestling with right now.

1. Start where your questions are

If you wonder about God's names ("LORD," "God," "Jesus," "Christ"), begin with Part II.

If you are unsure what the Bible means by "soul," "flesh," or "heart," try Part III.

If you want clarity on sin, salvation, grace, faith, righteousness, peace, go to Part IV.

If your questions are about hell, judgment, law, covenant, nations, look at Part V.

You don't have to follow the order. Use the Table of Contents like a map and choose a path that fits your current needs.

2. Read with a Bible open

Keep your regular Bible beside you (or open in an app).

For each chapter:

Read the short intro and look at the word box for the key terms.

Read the chapter, pausing when a passage is cited to actually look it up.

At the end, pick one of that chapter's passages and read it again, slowly, with the new word in mind.

The goal is not just to understand the word but to hear Scripture itself more clearly.

3. Use the tracks as "mini-courses"

The Parts are arranged as three main "tracks" plus some framing material:

Part II – The Name and Face of God

Part III – What Is a Human Being?

Part IV – Sin, Salvation, and the Good News

Part V – Time, Judgment, Law, and "Hell"

You can treat each track as a short course:

Read the Part introduction.

Work through its chapters over a few weeks.

Jot down one or two "this changes how I read..." notes at the end of each chapter.

Later, you can loop back and take a different track.

4. Keep advanced tools optional

Chapter 31 introduces practical tools (concordances, apps, interlinear features), but you do not need to use them for every passage.

A healthy rhythm:

Most days: simply read a chapter of Scripture and pray.

Sometimes: when a word stands out, use the tools from Chapter 31 to dig a little deeper.

Occasionally: follow one key word across a few passages, using the word index and glossary.

Let curiosity lead you rather than guilt. These tools are there when you want them; they're not homework.

5. Reading in groups

If you use this book with others:

Choose one track or a short cluster of chapters (for example, 11–13 on soul/spirit/body).

Before each meeting, everyone reads the chapter and one or two of the suggested passages.

In the group, focus on questions like:

"What did this word mean first?"

"How does that change how we hear this passage?"

"What difference could this make in how we live or pray?"

You don't have to agree on every detail. The point is to listen together and let Scripture shape you as a community.

6. When you feel overwhelmed

At any point, if you start to feel buried in terms:

Step back to something simple: a psalm, a parable, a section of a Gospel.

Read it in your own language with no tools.

Then, if you like, notice just one word and recall what you've learned about it.

You are not trying to carry every Hebrew and Greek term in your head. You are gradually training your ears so that, more and more, the Bible's own way of speaking can guide how you understand and follow it.

Who This Book Is For

This book is for ordinary Bible readers who sense that there is more going on under their English translation and want help hearing it without going to seminary.

It is for people who love Scripture but sometimes feel confused: Why does "soul" sound so ghost-like? Does "law" always mean the same thing? What exactly is "hell" in the Bible's own words?

It is for those who have heard bits of Hebrew and Greek—maybe in sermons or footnotes—and would like a clear, gentle guide that explains what matters without drowning them in grammar.

It is for small-group leaders, Sunday school teachers, and pastors who want simple, reliable ways to explain key terms to others without relying on shaky word tricks or internet rabbit holes.

It is for readers who are curious about different canons (Protestant, Catholic, Orthodox, Ethiopian) and want to know what difference, if any, those lists of books make for how we hear the Bible.

It is also for those who carry questions or doubts: about judgment, hell, salvation, or God's character, and suspect that part of their struggle comes from flattened or fuzzy translations.

This book is not only for experts. You do not need to know any Hebrew or Greek to benefit. If you can read an ordinary Bible and are willing to slow down, look carefully, and learn a few new terms along the way, this book is for you.

Part I

Why Words, Names, and Canons Matter

Books by Rene'

One Bible, Many Canons

Most of us talk about "the Bible" as if there were just one. We may notice different covers and translations, but we assume they all come from exactly the same list of books. Underneath, the story is a little more complicated—and more interesting.

This chapter is here to do one thing: show that when Christians say "Bible," they are talking about almost the same book, but not exactly the same **set of books**.

1. One New Testament we all share

Let's start with the easy part.

All major Christian groups—Protestant, Catholic, Orthodox, and others—agree on the same **27 New Testament books**. Matthew, Mark, Luke, John, Acts, Paul's letters, general letters, and Revelation are accepted everywhere.

That means whenever this book talks about the New Testament and its words for God, Jesus, or the church, you can relax: we are standing on ground that all Christians share.

2. Different Old Testament "libraries"

The differences show up in the **Old Testament**.

Think of three families living in three houses, each with a Bible on the table.

- In a **Protestant** home, that Bible has 39 Old Testament books.

- In a **Catholic** home, the Bible has those same books plus several more in the middle—books like Tobit, Judith, Wisdom of Solomon, Sirach, Baruch, and 1–2 Maccabees.

- In an **Orthodox** home, the Bible includes all of that, and then a few additional books again (depending on the tradition), such as 3 Maccabees or Psalm 151.

Every one of these families loves Jesus and calls their book "the Bible." They share the same New Testament and the same basic Old Testament story, but their Old Testament "libraries" are not identical.

It may help to picture this as three overlapping circles:

- The **middle** part—what all circles share—is the Old Testament you find in a Protestant Bible.

- The Catholic circle adds some books around that core.

- The Orthodox circle adds some more around that.

This book will stand in the middle and also look outward.

3. Why this matters for words and names

You might wonder: if the main story is the same, why does this matter for a book about words?

Because some of the words and ideas we care about—like **Wisdom, righteousness**, the **afterlife**, and even some pictures used for **Jesus**—are developed not only in the shared books but also in the extra ones.

For example:

- Books like **Wisdom of Solomon** and **Sirach** talk a lot about Wisdom, righteousness, and the fate of the righteous and the wicked. These ideas feed into how early Christians talk about Christ and about judgment.

- **1–2 Maccabees** tell stories of faithfulness under persecution and hint at resurrection hopes.

- Extra psalms and prayers in some Orthodox Bibles use familiar words like "soul," "spirit," "righteous," and "mercy" in ways that stand between the Old Testament and New Testament.

If we want to ask, "What did this word say first?" it sometimes helps to look, not only at the 39-book Old Testament, but also at these additional books many Christians have read as Scripture.

You do not need to start using a different Bible. You just need to know that when another Christian quotes "Wisdom" or "Sirach," they are drawing from a slightly different part of the family library.

4. How this book will handle the different canons

Here is the simple promise for the rest of this book:

- We will treat the **66 books** that Protestants use (and that Catholics and Orthodox also accept) as our main base.

- We will sometimes step into the **extra books** used by Catholic and Orthodox churches as helpful side rooms—places that show how certain words were used and understood between the Old and New Testaments.

- Whenever a passage comes from one of those extra books, it will be clearly marked, so you always know what you are looking at.

You do **not** have to agree on which books "should" be in the Bible to benefit from this. You simply need to be willing to see how Christians in different traditions have heard and used certain words.

5. The takeaway for you

By the end of this chapter, you only need to remember three things:

- Christians share **one** New Testament and **mostly** the same Old Testament.

- Different branches of the church include different extra Old Testament books.

- Those extra books sometimes help us understand how important words and names were used before the time of Jesus.

With that in mind, we can now turn to the next big question: how did those ancient words make their way into the English Bibles we hold today?

Chapter 2

From Scrolls to English

What Translation Does

None of the Bible was written in English. The Old Testament came to us in Hebrew and some Aramaic. The New Testament came in Greek. Every English Bible is a **translation**—a careful attempt to move meaning from one language into another.

This chapter is about what translation does, where it works beautifully, and where it can accidentally flatten important things.

1. Translation is about meaning, not just words

Imagine trying to translate these phrases into another language word-for-word:

- "It's raining cats and dogs."

- "My heart is broken."

- "He's on fire today."

If we translated those literally, we would confuse people. Good translation looks past the words and asks, "What do they **mean?**"

The same thing happens with the Bible. The people who translated it into English were not just swapping Hebrew and Greek words for English ones. They were trying to bring over the **sense** into a different time and culture.

That is already hard. Then add this: Hebrew and Greek often use concrete pictures and simple words where we might use abstract terms.

- Hebrew might say "his nose grew hot" where we would say "he was angry."

- Greek might use one word where we would use several.

Translators have to choose. In those choices, some of the richness can get flattened.

2. Different kinds of English Bibles

Not all translations are the same. You may have noticed that some feel "formal" and others feel "easy to read." Often, that difference comes from how they approach the task:

- Some try to stay as close as possible to the original wording and structure. These are sometimes called "word-for-word" or more **literal** translations.

- Others try to express the original idea in smooth, natural English, even if that means moving away from the original sentence structure. These are sometimes called "thought-for-thought" or more **dynamic** translations.

- Most fall somewhere in between.

Both approaches are useful. A more literal translation might help you see patterns or repeated words. A more dynamic one might help you feel the flow of the story in clear English. Neither one is perfect.

This book does **not** tell you which translation is "the best." Instead, it shows you that every translation is, by nature, a set of decisions—and that those decisions affect how we hear certain words.

3. How important words get flattened

Flattening happens when a rich, layered word in the original language is translated into one English word that carries only part of its meaning.

Here are a few examples we will explore later:

- Several very different words—**Sheol**, **Hades**, **Gehenna**, **Tartarus**—are sometimes all translated as **"hell."** Each of these words has its own picture and history.

- The word **ekklesia**, which means an assembly or gathering, is usually translated **"church."** For many readers today, "church" means a building or a Sunday service. The sense of "a people gathered around God" can fade.

- The Hebrew word **nephesh** and the Greek word **psychē** are often translated **"soul."** In many English-speaking minds, "soul" means a ghost-like part that lives inside the body. In the Bible, these words usually refer to the **whole living person**, not just an invisible piece inside.

Again, translators are not trying to trick anyone. They have to choose **some** English word. But if we never look under those choices, we may carry around thin, sometimes misleading ideas.

4. Translation across time and culture

Translation is not only about moving between languages; it is also about moving between **worlds**.

- The story of Moses and Pharaoh was first heard by people who knew the smell of mud bricks and the fear of powerful kings.

- The visions of Daniel were first heard by people living under foreign empires, trying to stay faithful in a strange land.

- Paul's letters arrived in bustling cities filled with temples, markets, and many competing ideas.

We hear those same texts today with smartphones in our pockets and different worries in our heads. That distance in time and culture means that even when a word is translated accurately, we may imagine something very different.

Part of the work of this book is simply to slow down and say, "In their world, what did this word most likely call to mind?"

5. What this book will do with translation

Here is what you can expect:

- This book will **not** argue that your Bible is unreliable.

- It will **not** spend pages comparing English translations.

- It **will** show you where English choices, even very understandable ones, can change how we picture God, Jesus, ourselves, and key ideas like "soul," "church," "hell," and "salvation."

Think of it this way:

Your English Bible is a very good window. This book helps you clean a few spots on the glass and notice what is on the other side.

By the end, you should feel more confident, not less, when you open your Bible—because you will know better what you are looking at.

Chapter 3

How to Read Word Studies Without Getting Lost

This whole book is built around words and names. That can be exciting—and also a little risky. If we are not careful, we can turn a helpful word study into a wrong idea. This chapter will give you a few simple "rules of the road" so you can enjoy the rest of the book safely.

1. One word, several meanings

Take the English word **"heart."** We use it in many ways:

- "My heart hurts." (feelings)

- "We live in the heart of the city." (center)

- "Take heart." (courage)

- "The surgeon operated on his heart." (literal organ)

If someone asked, "What is the one true meaning of 'heart'?", it would be hard to answer. The meaning depends on the **sentence**.

Biblical words work the same way. The Hebrew word **ruach** can mean wind, breath, or spirit. The Greek word **pneuma** can also mean wind, breath, or spirit. The right meaning comes from the **context**, not from a dictionary alone.

So when this book shows you the range of a word's meanings, remember: the point is not to find a secret "real meaning" you can plug into every verse. The point is to see what options are on the table, and then let the story choose.

2. Don't take words apart like math problems

Sometimes we hear that a Greek or Hebrew word is "made of two smaller words," and we are tempted to build meaning only from those parts. That can help, but it can also mislead.

In English:

- "Butterfly" is not "a fly made of butter."

- "Understand" is not "to stand under."

In the same way, knowing that ekklēsia comes from "out" (ek) and "call" (kaleō) doesn't mean its main meaning is "the called-out ones." In the Bible, ekklēsia is used for assemblies, gatherings, and meetings of people.

In this book:

- You will see word-parts when they are genuinely helpful.

- You will also see clear warnings not to lean too hard on them.

Enjoy word-parts as **illustrations**, not as magic codes.

3. How the word boxes work

Most chapters about words or names include one or two little "word boxes." Each one shows:

- The original word (in Hebrew or Greek letters).

- A simple spelling you can say out loud.

- A short meaning.

- A few key verses where the word is especially clear.

You don't have to memorize any of this. The boxes are there so you can:

- See that there really is a different word under your English term.

- Notice that the same original word appears in more than one place.

- Get a feel for how wide or narrow its meaning might be.

If you skip the boxes, you can still follow the chapter. If you read them, you'll have a clearer picture.

4. Tools you may already have

You might be surprised how much you can do with what you already have.

- A **study Bible** often has notes that say things like "Hebrew: nephesh" or "Greek: ekklēsia."

- Many Bible websites and apps let you tap on a word to see the underlying Hebrew or Greek and a simple definition.

- Comparing two or three different English translations can show you where translators struggled with a word.

You don't need anything fancy. The main tool is your **attention**.

5. How to use this book

Here is a simple way to get the most out of each chapter:

1. Read the **"Time and audience"** section. Ask: Who first heard this word? What were they going through?

2. Read the **Old Testament** side. Get a feel for how the word worked there.

3. Read the **New Testament** side. Notice what stays the same and what grows or changes.

4. Pay special attention to the **"Flattening"** section. That's where you see how English can shrink or shift the meaning.

5. Try at least one of the **"Try it yourself"** exercises at the end.

You don't have to do this for every chapter. Even if you pick a handful of words that matter most to you—like "soul," "hell," "church," "grace," and "Son of God"—and walk through them carefully, you will start to read the Bible differently.

6. Looking ahead

Part I has set the stage. You now know:

- Different Christians use slightly different Old Testament collections.

- Every English Bible is a translation with strengths and limits.

- Words can be rich and flexible, and we need to handle them with care.

In the next part of the book, we start where the Bible itself starts: with **God's name and God's face**. We will look at YHWH and "LORD," at "I AM" and "Lord," and at what happens when those words meet a man named Jesus.

As we go, keep asking that same simple question: **What did it say first?**

Part II

The Name and Face of God

Books by Rene'

The Name of God

YHWH, "I AM," and LORD

The Name of God: YHWH, "I AM," and LORD

When you open most English Bibles, you quickly see the word **LORD** in all capital letters. It appears in famous lines like, "I am the LORD your God, who brought you out of Egypt." Many of us read right past it. It sounds like a respectful title, not a name.

In the original Hebrew, that word is far more personal. It is not just "Lord" as in "boss" or "ruler." It is God's own **name**. This chapter is about that name, how it connects to the mysterious phrase "I AM WHO I AM," how it shows up as "Lord" and "I am" in the New Testament, and how our English Bibles can both honor and hide it at the same time.

The guiding question, as always, is: **What did it say first?**

1. When and to whom the name was first revealed

To understand the name, we have to step into the story where it appears.

1.1. Moses and a burning bush

The key scene is in Exodus 3. Moses is watching sheep in the wilderness when he sees a bush that burns but is not consumed. God calls to him from the bush and tells him to go back to Egypt to confront Pharaoh and lead Israel out of slavery.

Moses is understandably afraid and unsure. One of his questions is simple and practical: **"If I go and tell them that the God of their ancestors sent me, and they ask, 'What is his name?' what do I say?"** The people of Egypt and the surrounding nations have many gods, each with names and stories. Moses wants to know: who is sending me?

God answers with words that have puzzled and fascinated readers for centuries.

1.2. The first hearers

The first people to hear this name were not philosophers or theologians. They were **enslaved families** in Egypt, crying out for help. When God speaks His name in this setting, He is not giving Moses a puzzle to solve; He is giving a **promise** and a **relationship**. The name is tied to what He is about to do: bring His people out, defeat their oppressors, and make a covenant with them.

Later, Israelites will carry this name through wilderness, war, exile, and return. But its first sound rings out beside a burning bush and in the ears of a people desperate for rescue.

2. The four letters: YHWH in the Hebrew Bible

In Hebrew, God's personal name appears as four consonants: **Y-H-W-H**. Because it has four letters, scholars often call it the **Tetragrammaton**, which simply means "four-letter name."

2.1. How it looks in our Bibles

In the Hebrew Old Testament, these four letters show up thousands of times. They stand in sentences like:

- "YHWH said to Moses..."

- "Blessed be YHWH, the God of Israel..."

- "I am YHWH your God..."

In most English Bibles, this name is not printed as "YHWH." Instead, translators follow a long Jewish and Christian tradition of writing **LORD** in **small capital letters** whenever the Tetragrammaton appears. That is why you see "LORD" in verses where the Hebrew has YHWH, and "Lord" (normal capitalization) where the Hebrew has a different word, **Adonai**, meaning "master" or "lord." Scholars of the Hebrew Bible and Jewish tradition agree that this practice of **avoiding the spoken name** and substituting "Lord" developed over time, especially around and after the Babylonian exile, out of deep reverence for the name and a desire not to profane it.

When you see **LORD** in your Old Testament, you are looking at a place where the original text has the personal name **YHWH**.

2.2. Why we are not sure how to say it

In ancient times, Hebrew was written mostly with consonants. Native speakers knew how to supply the vowels. Later, when Jewish scholars added vowel marks to the text to preserve pronunciation, they often placed around YHWH the vowels for the substitute word "Adonai," to signal that readers should say "Lord" rather than the name itself. Because of this, and because the name was rarely spoken aloud for generations, its exact ancient pronunciation is uncertain.

Many scholars think **"Yahweh"** is close, based on comparative Semitic studies and ancient transcriptions. Others offer slightly different reconstructions. For our purposes, what matters most is not the exact sound, but the **role** of the name: God's personal covenant name, used when He acts and speaks as the One who brought Israel out of Egypt.

3. "I AM WHO I AM": understanding Ehyeh Asher Ehyeh

When Moses asks for God's name in Exodus 3, God responds with a phrase in Hebrew: **"Ehyeh asher ehyeh."** English Bibles usually translate this as:

- "I AM WHO I AM," or

- "I AM WHAT I AM," or

- "I WILL BE WHAT I WILL BE."

Scholars agree that this phrase is closely related to the divine name YHWH and to the Hebrew verb for "to be." They debate exactly how to bring out its meaning in English, but several important points are widely recognized.

3.1. A verb of "being" with a future flavor

The word **ehyeh** is a form of the verb "to be" in Hebrew. In this form, it can carry both present and future sense. That is why some scholars and translations lean toward "I WILL BE WHAT I WILL BE" rather than only "I AM WHO I AM." In context, as God promises to be with Moses and with Israel, many interpreters see the phrase as stressing **God's ongoing, faithful presence**—"I will be with you," "I will be who I will show myself to be"—rather than only making an abstract statement about existence.

Detailed studies of Exodus 3:11–18 point out that the name is explained within the story as something to be **remembered** and **called upon**, and that it appears in a context of God promising to act for Moses and Israel. This suggests that the name is not only about God's inner nature but about His **commitment to intervene** for His people in history.

3.2. How the phrase and the name go together

In the story, God first says to Moses, "Ehyeh asher ehyeh," and tells him, "Say to the Israelites: 'Ehyeh has sent me to you.'" Immediately after, God adds,

"Say to the Israelites, 'YHWH, the God of your fathers, has sent me to you.'
This is my name forever."

Scholars across Jewish and Christian traditions notice this deliberate pairing.
The phrase "I AM / I WILL BE" explains the name, and the name identifies
the One who is speaking. The connection is likely that YHWH is understood
as a form related to "He is / He will be," with "Ehyeh" as the first-person
version, "I am / I will be." On this reading, God is saying something like:

"I am the One who will be with you. That is who I am, and my name is 'He
is / He will be'—YHWH."

While some theological writings read "I AM WHO I AM" mainly as a statement about God as self-existent "Being," more recent work has pushed back
against seeing Exodus 3:14 as a purely philosophical claim. Many modern
scholars emphasize instead that, in this passage, the name functions as a
relational and narrative marker—it points to God's willingness to be
present and active with Moses and Israel, not just to timeless existence.

3.3. What English can miss

When English readers see "I AM WHO I AM," we may instinctively think
of a philosophical God who simply "is," beyond time and change. There is
truth in saying God simply "is," but if we stop there, we risk missing the
down-to-earth promise in the story: the God who **sees** the suffering of His
people, **comes down** to rescue them, and **goes with** Moses back to Egypt.

For the first hearers, "I AM / I WILL BE" would have sounded less like a
riddle and more like a pledge: "I will be there. I will be who I show myself to
be as I act for you."

4. From YHWH to LORD: a tradition of reverence—and a loss of clarity

Over time, Jewish readers treated the divine name with growing reverence. Out of respect and caution, they avoided pronouncing it in ordinary speech. Instead, when they read the Scriptures aloud and saw YHWH, they would say **"Adonai"**: "Lord," "Master."

By the last centuries before Christ, this practice was well established. Written sources from Jewish tradition explain that the name was not to be spoken casually and that the substitute "Lord" became standard in synagogue reading. This habit affected how the Hebrew Bible was copied and later translated.

4.1. The Greek Old Testament: Kyrios in place of the name

When Jewish translators produced a Greek version of the Hebrew Scriptures (often called the **Septuagint**), they often wrote **Kyrios**, the Greek word for "Lord," where the Hebrew text had YHWH. There is evidence that some early Greek manuscripts preserved the Tetragrammaton itself, but the dominant pattern in the main Old Greek tradition is that **Kyrios** functions as the written replacement for the name.

Scholars of the Septuagint have studied this pattern closely. Many conclude that, in these contexts, Kyrios often behaves less like a general noun and more like a **name-substitute**—that is, it is "treated as if it is a name," standing where YHWH stands.

4.2. English Bibles follow the same path

Most major English translations follow this long tradition:

- They print **LORD** (small caps) where the Hebrew has YHWH.

- They print **Lord** (normal) where the Hebrew has Adonai.

- They use **Lord** for Kyrios in the New Testament.

This convention is meant to balance faithfulness to the text with reverence for the divine name. It lets readers see that something special is going on (if they notice the small caps) without constantly confronting a form like "Yahweh," which many Christians are not used to.

But it also has a cost: for many readers, "LORD" and "Lord" blur together. The difference between God's **name** and God's **title** disappears. The sense that God gave Israel His personal name as part of a covenant relationship fades into a vague impression that "Lord" is just a formal way to talk about God.

5. "Lord" for God and Jesus in the New Testament

By the time of Jesus and the apostles, Greek-speaking Jews were used to hearing and reading **Kyrios** where their Scriptures referred to YHWH. At the same time, Kyrios was also the normal Greek word for "lord," "master," or "sir" in everyday life.

When the New Testament writers call Jesus **"Lord" (Kyrios)**, those two layers are both present:

- On one level, "Lord" can mean **Master** or **Ruler**, someone with authority.

- On another level, especially when the writers quote or allude to Old Testament texts, "Lord" can carry the weight of the divine name from Scripture.

Scholars who study early Christian views of God have pointed out that, in several key passages, Old Testament verses about YHWH are quoted or echoed in contexts that clearly refer to Jesus. For example, promises that "everyone who calls on the name of YHWH" will be saved are used in the New Testament as promises that everyone who calls on the **name of the Lord**—Jesus—will be saved. In Greek, the same word Kyrios is doing both jobs.

In English, "Lord" appears in both places. Unless we are paying attention, we may not realize that a verse is applying language about YHWH to Jesus.

6. Jesus and "I am" in the Gospel of John

The connection between Jesus and the divine name is especially strong in the Gospel of John. In several places, John has Jesus use the simple Greek phrase **"ego eimi"**—"I am"—in ways that recall how God speaks in the Greek Old Testament.

6.1. Ordinary and "absolute" uses

Sometimes "I am" in John is part of a normal sentence: "I am the bread of life," "I am the good shepherd," "I am the way, the truth, and the life." These are important, but they are clearly metaphors.

Other times, the phrase stands **almost alone**, with no obvious object:

- "Unless you believe that **I am**, you will die in your sins."

- "When you have lifted up the Son of Man, then you will know that **I am**."

- "Before Abraham was, **I am**."

These "absolute" uses (where "I am" is not followed by a "something") sound unusual. They echo how God speaks about Himself in certain Greek Old Testament passages, where He says "I am" in a strong, declarative way—especially in places where He contrasts Himself with idols and asserts His unique identity.

Some scholars argue that John is deliberately drawing on that Old Testament language. Others are more cautious. But there is broad agreement that, in John's narrative, these "I am" statements carry **heavy theological weight** and are part of how the Gospel presents Jesus as sharing in the identity and authority of Israel's God.

6.2. How Jesus' listeners react

In John 8:58, after Jesus says, "Before Abraham was, I am," the crowd picks up stones to throw at Him. That is not a normal reaction to someone making a confusing statement about age or existence. It is the reaction of people who hear in His words a claim that touches on the divine realm.

For listeners steeped in the Scriptures, a human being speaking in the kind of "I am" language used by God in passages like Exodus 3 and certain parts of Isaiah would sound dangerously close to claiming a divine status. This helps explain both the hostility Jesus faces and the strong reactions in the Gospel.

6.3. What English can smooth over

In English, "I am" is so common that we might read these verses without noticing anything special. The link back to "I AM / I WILL BE" in Exodus 3 is easy to miss, especially if we are not used to thinking about that phrase as tied to God's name and presence.

Part of this book's goal is simply to slow us down. When we see Jesus say "I am" in certain ways, we can ask: "Is this just ordinary speech, or is this one of those moments where the Gospel is hinting at something more? What did it sound like to people who knew Exodus and the prophets?"

7. What did it say first—and what do we hear now?

If we step back and look at the whole picture, we can see several things clearly:

- In the Old Testament, **YHWH** is God's personal name, revealed in the context of rescue and covenant. It is tied to the promise "I AM / I WILL BE," which, in the story, means God will be **with** His people and act for them.

- Out of reverence, Jewish readers chose to say "Lord" instead of pronouncing the name, and the Greek translation of the Scriptures usually used **Kyrios** in its place.

- Most English Bibles follow this tradition, printing **LORD** for YHWH and "Lord" for Adonai and Kyrios, which can make it hard for readers to see when the text is using a **name** and when it is using a **title**.

- The New Testament freely uses "Lord" for both God and Jesus. In some key passages, it uses Old Testament language about YHWH to speak of Jesus, and in the Gospel of John, it uses "I am" in ways that echo how God speaks of Himself in Scripture.

In other words, when we read "LORD" in our Old Testament and "Lord" and "I am" in certain New Testament verses, we are standing in the middle of a long and careful chain of translation and reverence. There is great beauty in that tradition; there is also some **flattening**.

We do not need to throw away our English Bibles. We simply need to remember, as we read, that behind "LORD" stands a **name**—and behind some of Jesus' "Lord" and "I am" statements stands the bold claim that the God who spoke from the burning bush is now speaking and acting in human flesh.

8. Try it yourself

To help the ideas in this chapter sink in, here are a few simple steps you can take with your own Bible:

1. Mark the name

- Pick a familiar Old Testament passage (for example, Exodus 3, Exodus 20, or a psalm).

- Every time you see **LORD** in small capitals, lightly write "YHWH" above it in pencil.

- Read the passage aloud, saying "Yahweh" or simply "the Name" where it appears, and notice how that changes the feel.

1. **Connect "I AM" and "I am"**

- Read Exodus 3:11–15 and pay attention to "I AM / I WILL BE" and "YHWH."

- Then read John 8:24, 28, and 58, noting how Jesus uses "I am."

- Ask: If I had grown up hearing Exodus in synagogue, how might these sayings strike me?

1. **Listen in worship**

- The next time you sing or say "Lord," pause and ask: am I addressing God with His covenant name in mind, or only thinking of a formal title?

- When you hear "Jesus is Lord," remember that in the New Testament world, this confession connects Him with the One Israel knew as YHWH.

The point is not to become obsessed with pronouncing the name correctly, but to deepen your sense that the God of the Bible is not a vague higher power. He is the One who told Moses His name, promised to be with His people, and, Christians confess, walked among us in Jesus.

Chapter 5

God, gods, and "the Lord"

Elohim and Adonai / Kyrios

Open any English Bible and you will find the word **"God"** on the first page: "In the beginning God created the heavens and the earth." A few lines later, you may also see **"the LORD"** or **"the Lord God."** For many readers, these words blur together. "God" is God, "Lord" is just another way of saying the same thing.

In the original languages, the picture is richer. The Hebrew Bible uses different words to talk about the one true God, about other "gods," and about God's role as "Lord" or "Master." The Greek Old Testament and the New Testament then use **Kyrios** ("Lord") in ways that link Israel's God and Jesus. Our English Bibles rightly use "God" and "Lord," but sometimes flatten important differences and connections.

This chapter looks at three key words:

- **Elohim** – usually translated "God."

- **Adonai** – usually translated "Lord."

- **Kyrios** – the Greek word "Lord," used in both Old and New Testaments.

We will keep asking: **What did these words say first, and what do we hear now?**

1. Elohim: "God" in the singular and "gods" in the plural

In Hebrew, the common word translated "God" in Genesis 1:1 is **'elohim**. It is a fascinating word, because it looks plural but often behaves grammatically like a singular when used of the God of Israel.

1.1. A plural form with a singular meaning

Hebrew nouns that end in **-im** are normally plural. *Elohim* is the plural form of *'el* or *'eloah*, words that can mean "god" in a general sense. When the Bible talks about foreign gods, idols, or "the gods of the nations," it also uses *'elohim* in a clearly plural way. In those cases, the surrounding grammar (plural verbs and adjectives) makes it obvious that "gods" is the right translation.

But when *'elohim* refers to the God of Israel, it normally takes **singular** verbs, adjectives, and pronouns. In Genesis 1:1, the verb "created" is singular. The sentence is not "the gods created"; it is "God created." This pattern runs throughout the Hebrew Bible. Scholars often describe *'elohim* in this usage as "plural in form but singular in meaning."

Think of English words like "news" or "mathematics." They look plural but function as singular. Something similar is happening with *'elohim* when it names the one Creator God.

1.2. "God" as a job description and a name

In many passages, *'elohim* is not just a label; it hints at a **role**. Some Jewish writers describe "Elohim" as something like a "job description" for the One who has supreme power and authority. When the Bible says, "In the beginning *Elohim* created," it is saying that the One who fills the role of true God brought everything into being.

At the same time, for Israel, *Elohim* is not just a category. It becomes one of the main **ways they refer to their God**. Alongside the personal name YHWH (often printed "LORD"), *Elohim* is used often in worship, prayer, and storytelling.

Because of this, English translations usually render *'elohim* as "God" when it clearly refers to Israel's God, and as "gods" when it clearly refers to other beings or idols.

1.3. What English "God" hides and reveals

The word **"God"** in English does a lot of good work:

- It signals the one supreme Creator and Ruler of all.

- Most readers intuitively understand that "God" in the Bible is not just any god.

But "God" is also **flat**:

- It does not show that the same Hebrew word *'elohim* can also refer to other "gods" or heavenly beings in some texts.

- It does not alert us to moments where the biblical writers contrast "our God" with other *elohim*—real spiritual powers or empty idols, depending on the passage.

If we only ever see "God" in the singular, we might miss the Bible's insistence that the Lord is **God of gods**, the true Elohim over every other claimed elohim. This matters for understanding Israel's faith in one God in a world full of rival spiritual claims.

2. Adonai: "Lord" as master and covenant ruler

Alongside *Elohim*, the Hebrew Bible often uses the word **'Adonai**. This is typically translated **"Lord"** (with normal capitalization). Where *'elohim* speaks of God as **God**, *'adonai* speaks of Him as **Lord**—the one who rules, commands, and cares for His people.

2.1. "Lord" in everyday life

In Hebrew, forms of *'adon* ("lord") can be used for human masters and important people. Servants might call their employer "my lord." Subjects might address a king that way. The plural intensive form *'adonai* becomes, in practice, a respectful way of speaking to God—"my Lord" or "my Master" in a supreme sense.

When the Bible says things like "O Lord, our Lord, how majestic is your name," or "Lord, hear my prayer," the underlying word is often *'adonai*. It expresses both respect and trust: God is the one in charge, the One whose will matters.

2.2. Adonai as a spoken substitute for the divine name

As we saw in the previous chapter, over time Jewish readers chose not to pronounce the name YHWH in normal reading. When they saw the four letters, they would say **"Adonai"** instead. This practice grew out of reverence and caution. In synagogue reading, the written name and the spoken substitute went together.

This has two important effects for us:

- It cements "Lord" language as one of the main ways people relate to God in prayer and worship.

- It sets up a pattern where, in some places, *Adonai* is the written word, and in others, it is the spoken replacement for YHWH.

Most English Bibles reflect this by printing:

- **LORD** (all caps) for YHWH, the divine name.

- **Lord** (normal) for *Adonai*.

Many readers never notice the difference. For them, "Lord" is just a formal religious word for God. But behind that one English word stand two different Hebrew words—one a **name**, one a **title**.

3. Kyrios in the Greek Bible: "Lord" as the bridge

When the Hebrew Bible was translated into Greek (the Septuagint), the translators had to decide what to do with *Elohim*, *Adonai*, and YHWH. For *Elohim*, they could use **Theos**, the normal Greek word for "god." For *Adonai* and YHWH, they typically used **Kyrios**, the Greek word for "Lord."

3.1. Kyrios for YHWH

Studies of the Septuagint show that in most books, forms of **Kyrios** appear where the Hebrew has the divine name YHWH. In some early manuscripts, the Tetragrammaton appears directly, but the main stream of Greek Old Testament manuscripts uses Kyrios as the **standard written substitute** for the name.

For Greek-speaking Jews, this meant that when they heard or read "Kyrios" in Scripture, they often understood it as a reference to the God of Israel—the One whose name their ancestors would have spoken as YHWH and later as "Adonai." In many contexts, Kyrios functioned almost like a **proper name** for God, even though it was also a common noun.

Scholars who have traced the use of Kyrios in the Septuagint note that this habit made it very natural, later on, for early Christians to use the same word for Jesus and for God the Father, with an overlap of meaning: "Lord" as title, and "Lord" as a stand-in for the divine name.

3.2. Kyrios for Adonai and human lords

Kyrios also serves as the Greek equivalent for Hebrew *'adonai* ("Lord") and for other uses of "lord" referring to human masters or respected figures. In Greek:

- A slave might call his master kyrios.

- A polite address might be "kyrios" ("sir").

So in the Greek Bible, Kyrios covers:

- The divine name (YHWH).

- The title "Lord" for God.

- The title "lord" for human beings.

That is a wide range. Once again, context has to tell us which sense fits each occurrence.

4. "Lord" in the New Testament: God and Jesus

By the time of the New Testament, the word **Kyrios** is ready-made to do double duty. It is already the word used in Greek Scripture for YHWH and for "Lord." Now the first Christians, who believe that Jesus is God's Messiah and more, begin to call Him "Lord" as well.

4.1. "Jesus is Lord": more than a slogan

When Paul says, "If you confess with your mouth, 'Jesus is Lord,' and believe in your heart that God raised him from the dead, you will be saved," the Greek word behind "Lord" is **Kyrios**. On the surface, that means "Jesus is the Master," "Jesus is the One in charge." But for people who know the Scriptures in Greek, it also resonates with passages where **Kyrios** stands in for YHWH.

Some scholars have argued that the long history of using Kyrios for the divine name "paved the way" for the New Testament writers to speak of Jesus and God in overlapping terms, sometimes quoting Old Testament "YHWH verses" and applying them to Jesus. When they say "Jesus is Lord," they can mean both "Jesus is my Master" and "Jesus shares in the identity of the Lord of Israel."

In English, "Jesus is Lord" is a familiar confession, but we often hear only the "Master" side. The connection back to YHWH and "the Lord" of the Old Testament is easy to miss.

4.2. Lord for God, Lord for Jesus, one English word

The New Testament uses **Kyrios** in several ways:

- For God the Father, sometimes echoing Old Testament passages about YHWH.

- For Jesus, as a confession of His authority and divine status.

- For the Holy Spirit in a few places.

- For human masters or as a polite form of address.

English Bibles translate almost all of these simply as **"Lord."** Without notes or careful reading, it can be hard to tell:

- When "Lord" means "God (the Father)" as in the Old Testament.

- When "Lord" refers specifically to Jesus.

- When "Lord" means a human master or "sir."

Some study Bibles use different capitalization or context clues to help. But for many readers, "Lord" in the New Testament becomes a **single flat word**, and the rich pattern of connections—to YHWH, to Adonai, to Israel's

Scriptures—fades into the background.

5. How English "God" and "Lord" flatten the picture

Our English Bibles have to choose some words. **"God"** and **"Lord"** are the natural choices. They are not wrong. But if we never look underneath them, we may miss several important things:

1. **"God" hides the flexibility of Elohim.**

- The same Hebrew word can refer to the one true God or to other claimed gods.

- The Bible's claims about God's uniqueness often sit right beside mentions of other *elohim* who are judged or dismissed. English "God" and "gods" show some of this, but we may not realize that the same root lies behind both.

1. **"Lord" hides the name-title distinction.**

- We lose track of when the text is using God's personal name (YHWH, printed "LORD") and when it is using a title (Adonai, "Lord").

- We may not notice when a New Testament "Lord" quotation is actually pulling a YHWH passage from the Old Testament and applying it to Christ.

1. **"Lord" hides the bridge built by Kyrios.**

- The same Greek word is used for the God of Israel in the Greek Old Testament and for Jesus in the New Testament.

- That overlap is part of how the New Testament is saying, "The one you knew as 'the LORD' has now acted and spoken in Jesus."

None of this means English Bibles are untrustworthy. It simply means that "God" and "Lord" do more work in translation than we often realize. Seeing what is under them can make our reading sharper and more worshipful.

6. What did it say first—and how should we listen now?

When ancient Israelites heard **Elohim**, they heard both a claim and a contest. Their Scriptures lived in a world where many *elohim* were worshiped, but the story insists: **YHWH is Elohim** in a unique way—the Creator, the covenant God, the one above all others.

When they prayed to **Adonai**, they spoke to their Lord and Master, the One who had every right to command and every reason to protect. When they heard **YHWH**, they thought of the God who brought them out of Egypt and gave them His name.

When Greek-speaking Jews and early Christians heard **Kyrios** in Scripture, they heard the Lord of Israel. When they confessed "Jesus is Kyrios," they heard far more than "Jesus is my boss." They heard the claim that Jesus shares in the identity and authority of the God they had worshiped as "the LORD."

Today, when we read "God" and "Lord" in English, we stand at the end of that long line. If we remember what these words carried at the start, we will read more carefully:

- When we say "God," we can remember the Creator and covenant God who stands over all other claims to divinity.

- When we say "Lord," we can remember God's name and title in the Old Testament and recognize the boldness of giving that same word to Jesus.

We do not need to become language experts. We just need to be willing to ask, now and then: **Behind "God" and "Lord" on this page, which word is**

hiding, and what story does it tell?

Try it yourself

Here are a few simple exercises you can try with your own Bible:

1. **God and gods in a commandment**

- Read Exodus 20:1–3 (the start of the Ten Commandments).

- Notice "God" in verse 2 and "gods" in verse 3.

- Remember that the same Hebrew root underlies both: *Elohim*.

- Ask: How does it change my sense of the verse to hear, "You shall have no other *elohim* before me"?

1. **LORD and Lord in a psalm**

- Read a psalm like Psalm 8 or Psalm 110 in a translation that marks **LORD** vs **Lord**.

- Mark each one with "YHWH" or "Adonai" above it.

- Notice when the psalm is using God's name and when it is using His title.

1. **Lord in the New Testament**

- Read Philippians 2:9–11 or Romans 10:9–13.

- Note how often "Lord" appears and who it refers to.

- If your Bible has cross-references, see which Old Testament verses are being echoed.

- Ask: What does it mean that words once spoken about YHWH are now spoken about Jesus?

As you keep reading, you may find that "God" and "Lord" feel less generic and more like what they were in the beginning: words that carry the weight of a living story between God and His people.

Chapter 6

The Name "Jesus"

Yeshua, Joshua, and "The LORD Saves"

Most of us hear the name **"Jesus"** so often that it feels like a pure label, almost like a brand. We forget that, in the world of the Bible, it was a **normal Hebrew name** with a clear meaning, a history, and a story already attached to it.

In this chapter we ask: What did the name **Jesus** say first? What did it sound like to the first people who heard it? And how does our English word "Jesus" quietly flatten some of that meaning?

1. The name before the manger: Joshua in the Old Testament

Long before Mary held a baby in Bethlehem, there was another man whose name sounded very much the same: **Joshua,** the successor of Moses.

1.1. Yehoshua: "YHWH is salvation"

In Hebrew, Joshua's name appears as **Yehoshua** (.)□□□□□□□□□□Scholars agree that this name is made from two parts:

- **Yeho-** – a shortened form that points to the divine name **YHWH.**

- **-shua** – from a verb meaning **"to save"** or **"to deliver."**

Put together, **Yehoshua** means something like **"YHWH is salvation," "YHWH saves,"** or **"YHWH is the one who saves."**

The Old Testament itself highlights this connection. In Numbers, Joshua is first called **Hoshea** ("he saves"), and Moses changes his name to **Yehoshua** by adding the element from God's name, making it clear that **the LORD**—not Joshua himself—is the true source of salvation. The name becomes a banner over Joshua's life and mission: he will lead God's people into the promised land, but it is **YHWH** who is saving and giving victory.

1.2. A shorter form: Yeshua

Over time, Hebrew names with "Yeho-" at the front often develop shorter forms. For Yehoshua, the shorter form is **Yeshua** (.)□□□□□□□□This shorter name appears in later Old Testament books (like Ezra and Nehemiah) and in related Aramaic texts. It still carries the same basic meaning: **"YHWH saves"** or "salvation."

Scholars who study these names point out that this shortening from **Yehoshua** to **Yeshua** happened **centuries before** the time of Jesus. In other words, people named "Yeshua" already lived in biblical times; it was not invented later.

So, by the time of the New Testament, **Yeshua** is a known, meaningful name in Jewish life—a shorter way of saying what **Yehoshua** said: **"YHWH saves."**

2. From Yeshua to Iēsous to "Jesus"

The New Testament was written in Greek. When the writers wanted to mention someone named Yeshua, they had to spell that name using the Greek alphabet and Greek sound patterns.

2.1. Iēsous: the Greek form

In Greek, the name appears as **Iēsous** (Ἰησοῦς). This is the standard way Greek writers represented the Hebrew/Aramaic name **Yeshua**. We can see this clearly in the Greek translation of the Old Testament (the Septuagint), where the book of **Joshua** is titled with that same form: **Iēsous**.

So in Greek:

- **Joshua son of Nun** is called **Iēsous**.

- **Jesus of Nazareth** is also called **Iēsous**.

It is the **same Greek name** applied to two different people at different times.

2.2. From Iēsous to Jesus

Our English word **"Jesus"** is a later transliteration of that Greek form. The path goes roughly:

Hebrew **Yehoshua** → shortened Hebrew/Aramaic **Yeshua** → Greek **Iēsous** → Latin **Iesus** → English **Jesus**

Each step adjusts the name to fit the rules of the language. For example, Greek masculine names often end in **-s**, so Yeshua becomes Iēsous. Latin and then English carry that form forward.

By the time we reach modern English, the name "Jesus" is very familiar—but we can no longer "see" in the English spelling that it is the same name as **Joshua**, and we cannot "hear" that it originally meant **"YHWH saves."**

3. "You shall call his name Jesus": Matthew 1:21

The Gospel of Matthew does something remarkable with this name. An angel appears to Joseph in a dream and says:

"You shall call his name Jesus, for he will save his people from their sins."

The angel is doing a word-play: **His name means "YHWH saves," and He will save.**

3.1. The name's meaning matches the mission

When Joseph hears "You shall call his name Yeshua" (or, in Greek, Iēsous), he does not hear an empty sound. He hears the familiar name that means "YHWH saves." The angel then explains **why** this is the right name: "because he will save his people from their sins."

Many scholars point out that this kind of explanation fits a world where names are often **chosen for their meaning**. It is as if the angel is saying:

"Name Him 'YHWH saves,' because He Himself will carry out YHWH's saving work."

This is not accidental. It signals that Jesus' life and death are not just good examples or strong teaching; they are the way God is acting to bring His people out of a deeper slavery—**slavery to sin and death.**

3.2. The Joshua echo

The name also quietly calls to mind **Joshua son of Nun**, the leader who brought Israel into the promised land after Moses' death. Some Christian writers and scholars have seen a pattern:

- Joshua (Yehoshua/Yeshua) led Israel into the land after the exodus.

- Jesus (Yeshua) leads God's people into a deeper, final "rest" and a new creation.

The New Testament letter to the Hebrews hints at this connection by comparing Joshua's rest with a greater rest still to come. Bearing the same name as Joshua, Jesus is presented as the one who finishes what earlier leaders could only begin.

In English, because we use different words "Joshua" and "Jesus," many readers never notice this echo. To someone hearing the story in Hebrew or in

Greek, the connection would be more obvious.

4. What our English "Jesus" flattens

The English name **"Jesus"** is not wrong. It faithfully carries the Greek form across centuries. But if we never look underneath it, we miss at least three important things.

4.1. We miss the meaning: "YHWH saves"

Most English readers do not automatically think "YHWH saves" when they hear "Jesus." The name has become a label, a sound, a religious word. The built-in message that God saves is hidden.

When Matthew tells us why the child must be named Jesus—"for he will save his people from their sins"—he is making that meaning explicit. If we heard the story in Hebrew, we would feel the punch more quickly. The name and the mission line up perfectly.

4.2. We miss the connection to Joshua

Because English uses two different names, "Joshua" for the Old Testament figure and "Jesus" for the New Testament one, we rarely think of them together. Yet in Greek, they share the same name. And in Hebrew, the forms Yehoshua and Yeshua are closely related.

The result is that many modern readers do not realize that:

- When the New Testament mentions "Joshua," it is using the same Greek form as "Jesus."

- The story of Joshua entering the land is part of the backdrop for understanding Jesus' role as the one who brings God's people into their full inheritance.

Our ears do not catch that echo automatically. We have to be told.

4.3. We may miss how bold the name really is

If only **YHWH** can truly save, and if the child's name means "YHWH saves," and if that child is the one who actually saves people from their sins, then there is a strong claim tucked into the name itself about **who Jesus is**.

Early Christians, reading Matthew 1:21 alongside other Scriptures, saw in this name not just a job (savior) but a statement about identity: the saving work of YHWH is happening in and through this person. When we treat "Jesus" as a simple label without meaning, we may not feel the weight of that claim.

5. Time and audience: how the name would have sounded then

It helps to pause and imagine what the name "Jesus" (Yeshua) would have sounded like to different people in the first century.

- To **Joseph and Mary**, it is a familiar, meaningful Jewish name, given by God's command. They know its meaning: **"YHWH saves."**

- To their **neighbors**, it might first sound like any other child's name. But as stories spread of what this Jesus is saying and doing—healing, forgiving sins, casting out demons—the name's meaning becomes more and more pointed.

- To the **disciples**, who come to believe that Jesus is God's Messiah and more, the name becomes a constant reminder: God saves, and He does it through this man.

- To **Greek-speaking believers**, Iēsous is a name they can say in their own language, but behind it still lies the Hebrew and Aramaic meaning.

Today, for many of us, "Jesus" is so common that it can feel almost generic. Part of the goal of this chapter—and of this whole book—is to let some of that original sharpness back in.

6. What did it say first—and how can we hear it now?

When we ask, "What did the name Jesus say first?", the answer is simple and deep:

- It said **"YHWH saves."**

- It said, "God is the Savior," not "humans save themselves."

- It carried the memory of Joshua and the promise of a greater salvation.

- In Matthew's story, it said, "Name Him 'YHWH saves,' because He will save His people from their sins."

Our English Bibles keep the form "Jesus," which is fine. What we need is not a new spelling, but a **new awareness**.

We can train ourselves, gently, to think:

Whenever I hear "Jesus," I will remember: "The LORD saves."

That one simple habit can change how we hear the Gospels, how we read the cross, and how we talk about salvation. It protects us from thinking of Jesus mainly as a teacher, a moral example, or a religious founder, and re-anchors us in His basic identity: **He is the one through whom God saves.**

Try it yourself

Here are a few ways to let this chapter sink in:

1. **Rewrite Matthew 1:21 with the meaning showing**

- Take the verse and write it out in your own words, replacing "Jesus" with "YHWH saves."

- For example: "You shall call His name 'YHWH saves,' because He will save His people from their sins."

- Notice how much sense the explanation makes when you hear the meaning.

1. **Connect Jesus and Joshua**

- Read a few key scenes from the book of Joshua (for example, Joshua 1 and Joshua 3) and then read parts of the Gospels.

- Ask: How does Joshua leading the people into the land prepare us for Jesus leading people into something greater?

1. **Pray with the meaning in mind**

- The next time you pray "in Jesus' name," pause and include the meaning: "in the name of the One through whom YHWH saves."

- Let that guide what you ask and how you trust.

The name "Jesus" is not an empty label. It is a short sentence, a promise, and a confession. Learning to hear it that way is one important step in hearing the Bible's real story more clearly.

Suggested Sources for Further Study (Chapter 6)

You can place these in a consolidated reference list at the back of the book; they are grouped here by topic.

On the names Yehoshua, Yeshua, and their meanings

- Standard Hebrew name dictionaries and lexicons that derive **Yehoshua** from elements meaning "YHWH" and "salvation," yielding "YHWH is salvation / saves."

- Studies on the shortening of theophoric names (names containing "Yeho-" or "Yo-") and the development of the shorter form **Yeshua** in late biblical Hebrew and Aramaic.

- Articles and monographs that discuss the occurrence of the name Yeshua in books like Ezra and Nehemiah and in inscriptions.

On the Greek form Iēsous and the link between Joshua and Jesus

- Septuagint studies showing that **Joshua son of Nun** is called **Iēsous** in the Greek Old Testament, and that the same Greek form is used for **Jesus of Nazareth** in the New Testament.

- Works on New Testament onomastics (the study of names) that trace the path: Yehoshua → Yeshua → Iēsous → Jesus.

- Scholarly discussions of Hebrews and other New Testament writings that explore the typological connection between Joshua and Jesus.

On Matthew 1:21 and the theology of Jesus' name

- Academic commentaries on Matthew that highlight the word-play in 1:21 ("you shall call his name Jesus, for he will save his people from their sins") and discuss how the name's meaning supports Matthew's portrait of Jesus as the one through whom God saves His people.

- Articles focusing specifically on Matthew 1:21 that examine how the verse links Jesus' identity, His name, and His saving mission.

Chapter 7

Messiah and Christ

God's Anointed King

When you hear **"Christ"**, what comes to mind? For many people, it sounds like Jesus' last name: "Jesus Christ," as if "Christ" were like "Smith" or "Johnson." In the Bible's world, "Christ" is not a surname. It is a **title**. It translates a Hebrew word—**Mashiach**—that means **"anointed one."** That title is soaked in stories of oil poured on heads, kings chosen by God, and a long-growing hope that one day God's anointed king would come and put the world right.

This chapter asks: **What did "Messiah" and "Christ" say first?** Who were "anointed ones" before Jesus, what were people expecting in His day, and how does our English word "Christ" sometimes flatten that story?

1. Mashiach in the Old Testament: "Anointed One"

The Hebrew word **māshîach** ( )☐☐☐☐☐☐☐☐☐literally means **"anointed one."** It comes from a verb that means "to smear" or "to rub" oil on something or someone. In ancient Israel, anointing with oil was how God's people **set someone apart** for a special role.

1.1. Who got anointed?

In the Old Testament, three kinds of people are normally anointed:

- **Kings** – Israel's rulers were anointed with oil to mark them as chosen by God. Saul, David, and later kings are called "the LORD's anointed."

- **Priests** – Especially the high priest, who represented the people before God, was anointed.

- **Sometimes prophets** – A prophet like Elisha is commissioned in a way that echoes anointing.

The oil itself is not magic. It is a visible sign—a bit of **perfumed, sacred oil** poured on someone's head to say, "This person is set apart by God, with God's backing, for this task."

When someone is called "the LORD's *mashiach*," it means they are an **official, authorized servant**: a king, a priest, or occasionally another leader. The word by itself does not yet mean "the final Savior of the world." It means "the one God has anointed for this job."

1.2. Mashiach used for surprising people

We might expect "God's anointed" to refer only to Israelites. But at one point, the prophet Isaiah even calls a foreign ruler, **Cyrus, king of Persia**, God's "anointed" (mashiach). Cyrus is the one God uses to end the exile and let the Jewish people go home and rebuild. That does not make Cyrus a Jewish Messiah in the later sense, but it shows that "anointed one" can be used broader than we might think: **anyone God has chosen and empowered for a role** can, in some contexts, be called His mashiach.

This reminds us that the word "anointed" is not automatically a code word for "the final Messiah." It always has to be read in context: who is being anointed, and for what?

2. From Mashiach to Christos: the Greek "Christ"

When Jewish translators put the Hebrew Scriptures into Greek (the Septuagint), they needed a word for **mashiach**. They chose **christos** (χριστός), from a Greek verb meaning **"to anoint."**

So in the Greek Old Testament:

- When a king is called "the LORD's anointed," the Greek often says "the Lord's **christos**."

- When priests or others are described as anointed, forms of the same word appear.

In other words, **"Christ" is simply the Greek way of saying "anointed one."** There is nothing inherently "Christian" about the word at first. It is a title used in the Scriptures that the early church read.

When we move into the New Testament, this Greek word **christos** carries all that Old Testament baggage: kings, priests, oil, choosing, and God's seal of approval.

3. What people expected: Messiah hopes in Jesus' time

By the time of Jesus, many Jewish people were living under foreign rule—first the Greeks, then the Romans. They read their Scriptures and longed for God to send a **Mashiach** who would set things right.

Scholars who study writings from this period (sometimes called Second Temple Judaism) have found a **variety** of expectations:

- Some expected a **royal son of David** who would defeat enemies and rule in justice.

- Some imagined a **priestly figure** who would purify worship and lead the people in faithfulness.

- Some writings picture an almost **heavenly or cosmic figure**, called "my son" or a "son of man," who would judge and restore the world.

- Some seem to blend these ideas: a conquering yet righteous king, a wise leader, a judge, a restorer.

There was no single "official" picture of the Messiah that every Jewish person held. But there was a widespread hope that God would send **a figure from Himself** who would restore Israel, deal with enemies, and bring God's kingdom in a clear way.

Into that world, the New Testament writers start using the word **christos** in connection with Jesus.

4. "You are the Christ": Christ as a title in the Gospels and Acts

In the earliest Christian writings, "Christ" is clearly a **title**, not yet a name.

- The Gospel of Mark opens: "The beginning of the good news about **Jesus Christ, the Son of God**." The phrase is like "Jesus the Messiah."

- Peter confesses, "You are the Christ, the Son of the living God." He is saying, "You are the Messiah we've been waiting for."

- In Acts, preachers speak about "Jesus **the Christ**" and argue that "this Jesus whom I proclaim to you is the Christ."

In these contexts, "Christ" answers a **question**: "Is Jesus the anointed king we were hoping for?" The answer is yes. The title ties Him to the long line of anointed kings and to the prophecies about a coming ruler from David's line.

When first-century Jews heard "Jesus is the Christ," they did not think "this is His last name." They heard: "This is the one God has anointed as King, in line with the promises."

5. Christ as King, Priest, and Prophet

Early Christians quickly saw that Jesus fulfilled more than just **one** anointed role.

- As **King**, He proclaims and embodies the kingdom of God, rules by serving, and is said to be seated at God's right hand.

- As **Priest** (a theme especially strong in the letter to the Hebrews), He offers Himself as the perfect sacrifice and intercedes for His people.

- As **Prophet**, He speaks God's word with authority and reveals the Father.

In that sense, Jesus is the **Messiah who combines all the anointed roles**:

- He is the King who rules.

- The Priest who brings us near to God.

- The Prophet who tells the truth and calls for repentance.

Some classic Christian teaching explicitly says: "Christ" points to Jesus as **Prophet, Priest, and King**—the ultimate Anointed One who gathers up all earlier anointings in Himself.

Our English word **"Christ"** often carries these ideas only faintly. Many people hear "Christ" and think of a purely religious label without kingship, priesthood, or prophetic edge.

6. When "Christ" becomes a name

As the New Testament progresses, especially in Paul's letters, we start to see

"Christ" used more like a **name**:

- Phrases like "Christ Jesus" or simply "Christ" appear where we might expect "Jesus."

- In some contexts, "Christ" functions as a kind of shorthand: a way to speak about the crucified and risen Jesus who is Lord.

Scholars note a pattern: in the earliest layers, "Christ" is clearly a title ("the Christ"), but as Christian communities grow, the title becomes so closely attached to Jesus that it effectively **functions as part of His name**.

In English, this has gone even further. Many people say "Jesus Christ" as a fixed pair and assume "Christ" is His last name. We do the same when we speak of "Christians," "Christianity," "Christ-like," and so on.

There is nothing wrong with "Christ" functioning as a name—we can hardly avoid it now. The danger is forgetting that **underneath that name is a job and a story**: the story of God's anointed king and the job of ruling, saving, and restoring.

7. How "Messiah/Christ" gets flattened in English

Our English words **"Messiah"** and **"Christ"** are accurate translations of mashiach and christos, but they can easily be flattened in our minds.

Here are some common ways that happens:

7.1. Christ as a surname

When we think of "Christ" as Jesus' last name, we:

- Forget that it **announces His role**: the Anointed One.

- Lose the connection to the long line of anointed kings and priests in Israel's story.

- Stop asking the key question: "What kind of Messiah is He?"

7.2. Messiah as only "spiritual Savior"

Sometimes Christians talk as if "Messiah" means only "the one who saves my soul from hell." Salvation definitely includes forgiveness and eternal life. But in the Bible, Messiah is also:

- A **king** who brings justice.

- A **judge** who confronts evil.

- A **restorer** who renews creation.

- A **leader** who gathers a people.

If we shrink "Messiah" into a purely private, spiritual helper, we flatten the full kingly, public, world-shaping sense of the title.

7.3. Losing the Old Testament roots

Without the Old Testament background, "Christ" floats:

- We may not connect Jesus' title to promises made to David about a descendant who would reign forever.

- We may not see how His kingdom teaching uses language from prophets who dreamed of peace, justice, and the knowledge of God covering the earth.

When "Christ" is cut loose from that soil, it becomes a vague religious word rather than the heavy, rooted title it was meant to be.

8. What did it say first—and how can we hear it now?

When ancient Israelites heard **mashiach**, they saw oil shining on a head.

They saw a priest stepping into the tabernacle, a king taking the throne, a prophet set apart to speak for God. They heard: **"This person has been chosen and marked by God for a special role."**

When Jews living under foreign rule heard or read about **the** Mashiach to come, they heard hope: a king or leader from God who would put things right, defeat evil, restore Israel, and bring God's rule in a new way—even if they did not all agree on exactly how that would look.

When Greek-speaking Jews and first-generation Christians said **christos**, they meant the same thing: **"the anointed one."** When they called Jesus "the Christ," they were saying, "He is that Anointed One from God. He is the king. He is the one God has chosen and empowered."

Today, when we say **"Christ"**, we often think only of Jesus in a church context. To hear it the way they did, we can train ourselves to remember:

Whenever I see or say "Christ," I will think: **"the Anointed King," "God's chosen ruler," "the one God has set apart as Prophet, Priest, and King."**

That simple shift turns "Christ" from a thin religious label back into a thick, story-filled title.

Try it yourself

Here are a few ways to practice hearing "Messiah/Christ" as a title again:

1. **Add the meaning when you read**

- The next time you read "Jesus Christ" in your Bible, whisper the meaning in your mind: "Jesus the Anointed King."

- See how that changes the feel of the verse.

1. **Read a king's anointing story**

- Read 1 Samuel 16, where David is anointed. Pay attention to the oil, the Spirit of the LORD coming on him, and the idea of being chosen.

- Then read a Gospel scene where Jesus speaks about the kingdom of God. Ask: How is Jesus like an anointed king? How is He different?

1. **Look at a confession**

- Read Peter's confession: "You are the Christ, the Son of the living God."

- Replace "Christ" with "the Anointed King" and "Son of God" with "God's chosen king and representative."

- Notice the weight of what Peter is really saying.

As you keep reading, you may find that "Christ" and "Messiah" start to feel less like abstract words and more like what they were at the beginning: titles announcing that **God has chosen and anointed Jesus to reign, to redeem, and to restore.**

Chapter 8

Son of God

Israel, the King, and Jesus

"**Son of God**" is one of the most famous titles for Jesus. Many Christians hear it and immediately think, "Jesus is divine." That is true—but in the Bible's own world, the phrase **Son of God** was already busy doing several other jobs before it was applied to Jesus.

In the Old Testament, "son(s) of God" can refer to **angels**, to **Israel as a nation**, and to the **Davidic king**. In the New Testament, all of that background is still there, and then something more is added: Jesus as God's **unique** Son. This chapter explores what "Son of God" said first and how our English ears often skip straight to the end of the story.

1. Sons of God in the Old Testament: more than one use

The phrase "son(s) of God" shows up in more than one way in the Hebrew Bible and related literature. If we want to understand how early Christians heard "Son of God," we need to see these earlier uses.

1.1. Heavenly beings: "sons of God" as members of God's council

In some Old Testament passages, **"sons of God"** (or "sons of the gods") refer to **heavenly beings**—what we might call angels or members of God's heavenly court. For example:

- In Job, "the sons of God" come to present themselves before the

LORD.

- Certain Psalms and early Jewish writings use similar language for spiritual beings around God's throne.

Scholars generally agree that in these contexts, "sons of God" does not mean "biological offspring" but **members of God's heavenly court**, subordinate to Him yet belonging to His realm. The phrase marks them as **belonging to God's world**, not as independent deities equal to Him.

This use shows that "son of God" language can mark **association with God**—belonging to His sphere—but it does not yet mean "the one, unique divine Son."

1.2. Israel as God's firstborn son

In Exodus, God tells Pharaoh, "Israel is my firstborn son; let my son go, that he may serve me." Here, the "son" is not a single person but **the whole nation**. God claims Israel as His family:

- He has chosen them.

- He cares for them.

- He disciplines and leads them.

Later prophets echo this language, portraying Israel as a son who has gone astray or as a child whom God loves and will restore. In this sense, **"son of God" means "people in a special covenant relationship with God."**

1.3. The Davidic king as God's son

In key royal passages, God speaks of the king in "son" language. For example:

- In the promise to David in 2 Samuel 7, God says about David's descendant: "I will be to him a father, and he shall be to me a son."

- In Psalm 2, which celebrates God's king and His rule over the nations, God says to the king, "You are my son; today I have begotten you."

Here, "son" is not a statement about the king's biological origin; it is a **royal adoption formula**. The king is God's chosen representative. To call the king "son" is to say:

"You stand for Me. You rule under My authority. I back your reign."

Jewish and Christian interpreters have long seen passages like Psalm 2 as foundational for understanding "Son of God" as a **royal** title. It ties together kingship and sonship: the **king of Israel** is, in a special sense, **God's son**.

2. Second Temple hopes: "son of God" and the coming king

Between the Old Testament and the New Testament, Jewish writings and hopes develop. Scholars who read texts from this period (sometimes called Second Temple Judaism) have found that "son of God" language is sometimes used for expected future figures:

- Some texts picture a **Davidic king** whose rule will extend over the nations, echoing Psalm 2.

- Others speak of an **exalted or heavenly figure** who acts as God's agent in judgment and salvation.

- There are also ongoing uses of "son(s) of God" for angels and other heavenly beings.

This means that when someone in Jesus' day hears "Son of God," they may think:

- of a **kingly, messianic** figure,

- of a **special relationship** with God,

- and perhaps of a figure who, while still under God, reflects His glory in a unique way.

There is still strong commitment to **one God**. The phrase "Son of God" sits within that commitment. For many Jews, the idea of a truly divine "only-begotten" Son would be more controversial. But there is already a **trajectory** of sonship language moving toward a fuller, richer meaning.

3. "Son of God" on the lips of the New Testament

When we cross into the New Testament, we do not leave this background behind. Instead, the writers build on it.

3.1. A royal, messianic title

In the Gospels:

- The angel tells Mary her child will be called **Son of the Most High** and says God will give Him the throne of David.

- When Jesus is confessed as **"the Christ, the Son of God,"** the two titles go together: Messiah and Son of God as linked royal ideas.

- In John, Nathanael exclaims, "You are the Son of God; you are the King of Israel!" From his mouth, "Son of God" and "King of Israel" are essentially parallel phrases.

This shows that, at one level, calling Jesus "Son of God" means **"You are the Davidic king God promised."** It is a fulfillment word: He is the long-awaited royal Son whom God promised to David and spoke of in Psalm 2.

3.2. A unique relationship

But the New Testament does not stop there. Especially in passages like:

- "No one knows the Son except the Father, and no one knows the Father except the Son..."

- "This is my beloved Son, in whom I am well pleased."

We see that Jesus' sonship is **unlike anyone else's**.

Other "sons of God" (angels, Israel, kings) share a relationship by **grace and calling**. Jesus is presented as sharing a relationship by **nature and identity** that is deeper. Later Christian theology will describe Him as the **eternal Son**, the second person of the Trinity. But already in the Gospels, His sonship is:

- closer

- more intimate

- and more central than the "sonship" of any other figure

3.3. Son of God and the cross

The phrase also appears at kcy moments of Jesus' suffering:

- During the trial, the question becomes, "Tell us if you are the Christ, the Son of God." His answer leads to a charge of blasphemy.

- At the cross, a Roman centurion, seeing how Jesus dies, says, "Truly this was the Son of God."

Here, "Son of God" is not just an abstract title. It is tied to **obedience, suffering, and death**. The Son of God does not simply sit on a throne; He goes to a cross. That shocking combination—royal sonship and sacrificial death—is at the heart of the New Testament's message.

4. Flattening "Son of God" in modern ears

Our English phrase **"Son of God"** carries a lot of theological weight. That is good—but it can also lead us to flatten or skip important layers.

Here are some common ways we flatten it:

4.1. Jumping straight to "second person of the Trinity"

Christian teaching rightly confesses Jesus as fully divine, the eternal Son. But if we always jump instantly to that conclusion when we read "Son of God," we may:

- Miss the **royal, messianic** meaning the phrase has in many Gospel scenes.

- Overlook how the title ties Jesus to God's promises to David and to Psalm 2.

- Skip the way His sonship is tied to His **obedience** and **suffering** (He is the Son who does what Israel and its kings failed to do).

The answer is not to deny His divinity, but to let the earlier layers speak too.

4.2. Treating it as only a biological or genetic phrase

Sometimes people hear "Son of God" and think mainly of **physical begetting** or "divine DNA." The Bible uses son language more flexibly and richly:

- For heavenly beings.

- For a whole nation.

- For a king in a metaphorical, royal sense.

When "Son of God" is applied to Jesus, it brings together those strands in a deeper way. Reducing it to a crude biological picture ignores the symbolic, relational, and royal dimensions that matter so much in Scripture.

4.3. Forgetting the shared sonship of God's people

The New Testament also speaks of **believers** as sons and daughters of God, adopted into God's family in Christ. Jesus is the Son in a **unique** way; we become sons and daughters **by grace**. If we forget the wider use of "son of God" in Scripture, we may miss how:

- Jesus is both **our brother** and **our Lord**.

- Our own identity as children of God is grounded in His sonship.

Keeping the whole range in view helps us see how His unique Sonship creates room for ours.

5. What did it say first—and how can we hear it now?

If we look back across the chapter, we can summarize what "Son of God" said first in Scripture:

- It marked **heavenly beings** as belonging to God's realm.

- It named **Israel** as God's "firstborn son" in covenant.

- It described the **Davidic king** as God's adopted royal son, ruling under His authority.

- It helped shape Jewish hopes for a coming **Messiah** who would be a son in a special sense.

When the New Testament calls Jesus "Son of God," it builds on all of this and then stretches beyond it. Jesus is:

- The true Israel in one person—the obedient Son.

- The rightful Davidic king—the royal Son who fulfills God's promises.

- The one who shares an unmatched relationship with the Father—**God's unique Son**.

For us, hearing this title well means **not skipping any of those layers**. When you read "Son of God":

- Remember the **king** and the **psalm** that first used the phrase.

- Remember the **nation** called "my son" and the **angels** who serve in God's presence.

- And then remember that the New Testament says: **this** Son is more than any of them. He is the one in whom all those earlier sonships find their meaning.

Try it yourself

Here are a few steps you can take with your own Bible to let this chapter sink in:

1. **Read an Old Testament "son" passage**

- Read Exodus 4:22–23 and note how Israel is called God's firstborn son.

- Then read 2 Samuel 7 and Psalm 2, and mark places where the king is described as God's son.

- Ask: What does "son" mean in these contexts?

1. **Read a New Testament "Son of God" confession**

- Read Matthew 16:16 or John 1:49, where Jesus is confessed as "the Christ, the Son of God" or "Son of God, King of Israel."

- Replace "Son of God" with "God's royal Son, the King He promised." Notice the emphasis.

1. **Connect sonship and the cross**

- Read the account of Jesus' trial and crucifixion in one Gospel.

- Pay attention to where "Son of God" appears: in questions, in mockery, in confession.

- Ask: How does the cross reshape what "Son of God" means?

If you practice hearing "Son of God" as a **royal, covenant, and relational title**, you will begin to see more clearly how rich and layered the Bible's vision of Jesus really is.

Chapter 9

Son of Man

The Human One and Daniel's Vision

"**Son of Man**" is the title Jesus uses for Himself more than any other in the Gospels. Many of us have heard that "Son of God" points to His deity and "Son of Man" points to His humanity. There is some truth in that, but the Bible's own use of "son of man" is more layered and surprising.

In the Old Testament, "son of man" can simply mean **"human being"**. In the book of Daniel, it becomes part of a striking vision about a figure who receives authority and an eternal kingdom. In Jesus' own mouth, "the Son of Man" weaves these threads together: He is both **truly human** and the **exalted figure** who will suffer, rise, and judge.

This chapter asks: **What did "son of man" say first, and what does it say when Jesus uses it?**

1. "Son of man" as "human being" in the Old Testament

In Hebrew, the phrase **ben 'adam** ("son of man") and related expressions are often used as ordinary ways of saying "a human being" or "mere mortal."

1.1. A poetic way to say "a human"

In some psalms and wisdom texts, we find parallels like:

- "What is man (**'enosh**) that you are mindful of him, and the son of man (**ben 'adam**) that you care for him?"

Here, "man" and "son of man" are poetic pairs. They both mean **human beings** in general. The phrase "son of man" draws attention to our **frailty** and **smallness** compared to God.

Ancient Jewish interpreters and modern scholars agree that in these contexts, "son of man" is not a title. It is an idiom for "human creature," underlining the contrast between God's greatness and human weakness.

1.2. Ezekiel: "son of man" as a reminder of humanity

In the book of Ezekiel, the prophet is addressed by God again and again as **"son of man."** Nearly every time God speaks to him, He begins, "Son of man, stand on your feet," or "Son of man, say to the house of Israel…"

Here too, "son of man" means "human." God is reminding Ezekiel:

- You are a human messenger.

- You are small and frail compared to My glory.

- You speak for Me, but you are not Me.

Scholars note that in Ezekiel, the title emphasizes **Ezekiel's humanity and lowliness** in contrast to the visions of God's overwhelming glory. It is a way of saying, "You, human one."

So in much of the Old Testament, "son of man" simply says: **"human being," especially in contrast to God."**

2. Daniel 7: "one like a son of man"

The phrase takes on new power in **Daniel 7**, where the prophet sees a vision of beasts, thrones, and judgment.

2.1. The vision

In Daniel 7, Daniel sees four great beasts representing kingdoms. Then he sees "the Ancient of Days" (a picture of God) seated in judgment. After the beasts are judged, Daniel says:

"Behold, with the clouds of heaven there came one like a son of man, and he came to the Ancient of Days…"

This figure is **"like a son of man"**—that is, he appears **human**, not beastly. He comes with the **clouds of heaven**, a phrase often associated with divine activity. And to this figure is given:

- Dominion

- Glory

- A kingdom that will not pass away

- Service (or worship) from "all peoples, nations, and languages"

Scholars have wrestled with this passage for a long time. Some see the "one like a son of man" as a **symbol of God's people** (the "saints of the Most High") being vindicated. Others see a more **individual, exalted figure** who represents the people and is given authority by God. Either way, several points are clear:

- The figure is **distinguished from God** (the Ancient of Days) but closely associated with God's rule.

- He is **human-like**, in contrast to the beastly empires.

- He is given a **universal and everlasting kingdom**.

Later Jewish writings pick up this "son of man" figure and develop him as a powerful, sometimes heavenly, agent of God's judgment and restoration. Christians later see this passage as pointing ahead to Christ.

2.2. A new layer added to "son of man"

Daniel 7 adds something new to the simple "human being" use of "son of man":

- It keeps the **human aspect** ("like a human"),

- But it adds an **exalted, end-time role**: receiving kingship and judging.

So by the time of Jesus, "son of man" language can call to mind both:

- Regular humans (as in Ezekiel and the psalms), and

- This special, human-like figure in Daniel 7, associated with God's end-time rule.

3. "Son of Man" on Jesus' own lips

In the Gospels, **"Son of Man" is the main title Jesus uses for Himself.** He calls Himself "the Son of Man" far more often than "the Son of God." Scholars have noticed that in His mouth, the phrase tends to fall into three broad patterns:

- "Son of Man" and **His present mission**

- "Son of Man" and **His suffering and death**

- "Son of Man" and **His future coming in glory**

3.1. The Son of Man in His present mission

Sometimes Jesus uses "Son of Man" when talking about what He is doing

now, in His earthly ministry:

- "The Son of Man came to seek and to save the lost."

- "The Son of Man came not to be served but to serve, and to give His life as a ransom for many."

- "The Son of Man has authority on earth to forgive sins."

In these sayings, "Son of Man" highlights Jesus' **human presence** (He has "come") and His **authority** (to forgive, to serve as ransom). The phrase "came" hints at pre-existence; "Son of Man" echoes both His humanity and something larger.

3.2. The Son of Man who must suffer

In another cluster of sayings, Jesus says that the **Son of Man must suffer**:

- "The Son of Man must suffer many things... be killed, and on the third day be raised."

- "The Son of Man is going to be delivered into the hands of men, and they will kill Him."

Here, "Son of Man" is tied to His **rejection, suffering, and death.** The one who is "like a son of man" in Daniel 7 is given glory and a kingdom; Jesus insists that **His path to that glory runs through the cross.**

This combination would have been surprising. If some people expected a "son of man" figure as a glorious judge, the idea that the Son of Man must be rejected and killed before being exalted is shocking.

3.3. The Son of Man coming in glory

Finally, Jesus speaks of the Son of Man returning in glory:

- "You will see the Son of Man seated at the right hand of Power and coming on the clouds of heaven."

- "When the Son of Man comes in His glory, and all the angels with Him, then He will sit on His glorious throne."

- "Then they will see the Son of Man coming in the clouds with great power and glory."

These sayings echo **Daniel 7** directly: "coming with the clouds of heaven," receiving authority, judging the nations. Jesus is clearly identifying Himself with the human-like figure who comes before the Ancient of Days.

So in Jesus' self-use:

- "Son of Man" points to His **humanity**.

- It draws on **Daniel 7's** vision of an exalted figure who receives a kingdom.

- It ties that exalted role to a path of **service, suffering, and death.**

4. Why Jesus may have chosen this title

Scholars have discussed why Jesus preferred "Son of Man" as His self-title. There is no universal agreement, but several plausible reasons often surface:

1. **It is flexible.**

- The phrase can mean "human," which emphasizes His solidarity with us.

- It can point to Daniel 7's exalted figure, highlighting His future glory and authority.

1. **It was not yet a fixed "title" in His day.**

- Unlike "Messiah," which carried strong political expectations, "Son of Man" seems not to have been a widely used formal title for a known figure.

- This may have allowed Jesus to **fill it with His own meaning**, combining humanity, suffering, and glory.

1. **It linked His story to Scripture without handing opponents an easy slogan.**

- By using Daniel 7 language in His trial ("you will see the Son of Man seated at the right hand of Power and coming on the clouds"), He subtly but clearly claimed a role in God's plans that His hearers would recognize.

- Yet throughout His ministry, the phrase could still sound humble: "this human one," "this son of man."

Whether or not we can be certain of His motives, the effect is clear: "Son of Man" becomes a **rich, multi-layered title** that holds together humanity and exaltation, suffering and judgment.

5. How "Son of Man" gets flattened today

Our English phrase **"Son of Man"** can be easily flattened in at least two ways.

5.1. "Son of Man = just human"

Sometimes people treat "Son of Man" as if it simply meant, "Jesus is human." It does affirm His humanity, but in the Gospels, Jesus uses the phrase:

- When claiming authority to forgive sins.

- When predicting His resurrection.

- When describing His future coming in glory on the clouds.

Those contexts are not about **mere humanity**. They draw on Daniel 7 language about an exalted, human-like figure given a universal kingdom. To reduce "Son of Man" to "just human" is to miss the glory side.

5.2. "Son of Man = only a divine title"

On the other side, some explain "Son of Man" as only a way of saying "Jesus is divine." That also misses something. The phrase keeps His **humanity** in view:

- It is rooted in idioms that mean "human being."

- It highlights that the one who will judge is **like us**—a "human one"—yet exalted.

If we treat "Son of Man" only as a code for divinity, we risk downplaying that Jesus really became human, shared our weaknesses (without sin), and stood among us as one of us.

The Bible holds both together. "Son of Man" means:

- **Human one** (He truly shares our nature), and

- The human-like One from Daniel's vision who receives **authority, glory, and a kingdom.**

6. What did it say first—and how can we hear it now?

If we listen to the Bible's own use of the phrase, "son of man" says:

- In the psalms and Ezekiel: **you are human, God is God; remember your smallness.**

- In Daniel: **a human-like figure will receive a kingdom and share in God's rule.**

- In Jesus' teaching: **this human one will serve, suffer, die, rise, and come again in glory to judge.**

So when we see **"Son of Man"** in the Gospels, we can train ourselves to remember:

- This title keeps Jesus' **humanity** front and center: He is "the human one."

- This same "human one" is also the **exalted figure** of Daniel 7, entrusted with God's own authority.

- His path passes through **service and suffering** before reaching **glory and judgment.**

Holding all of that together keeps us from flattening Jesus into either "only divine, not really human" or "only human, not truly exalted." The title "Son of Man" insists that He is **both**: fully human and the human One who now sits at the right hand of God.

Try it yourself

Here are a few simple ways to work with this chapter in your own Bible reading:

1. **See "son of man" in its "human" sense**

- Read a psalm like Psalm 8 and mark where "son of man" appears.

- Replace it with "human being" and note how it emphasizes our smallness and God's care.

1. **Read Daniel 7 slowly**

- Read Daniel 7, especially verses 9–14 and 27.

- Note how the "one like a son of man" is distinct from God yet receives authority and a kingdom.

- Ask: How would this shape what I expect from someone who calls Himself "the Son of Man"?

1. **Walk through one Gospel's "Son of Man" sayings**

- Pick one Gospel (e.g., Mark) and underline every time Jesus says "the Son of Man."

- In the margin, mark each one as: (P) present mission, (S) suffering/death, or (G) future glory.

- Notice how all three themes braid together in Jesus' use of the title.

As you practice, "Son of Man" will start to sound less like a confusing church phrase and more like what it was from the start: a name that says, **"Here is the truly human one who will serve, suffer, and reign."**

Chapter 10

Word, Wisdom, and Immanuel

God With Us

The Bible uses many names and titles to say that **God is not far away**. He speaks, He gives wisdom, He promises to be "with us." In the Old Testament, we meet the **Word of the LORD**, **God's Wisdom**, and a child called **Immanuel**. In the New Testament, the Gospel of John opens with **the Word (Logos)** made flesh, and Matthew says Jesus' birth fulfills the promise of "Immanuel."

This chapter explores how those strands fit together: Word, Wisdom, and Immanuel as ways of talking about **God's presence**, and how our English words can sometimes make them sound thinner than they really are.

1. "The word of the LORD": God speaking and acting

In the Old Testament, the phrase **"the word of the LORD"** appears again and again:

- "The word of the LORD came to Abram…"

- "The word of the LORD came to Jeremiah…"

- "By the word of the LORD the heavens were made…"

In Hebrew, the word here is **dābār**, which can mean a **word**, a **message**, or even a **thing/matter**. When the Bible says "the word of the LORD came," it usually means more than a sound in the air. It's God Himself **breaking into history**:

- He **reveals** His will.

- He **creates** and **sustains**.

- He **confronts** and **comforts**.

Scholars who study this phrase point out that "the word of the LORD" often acts almost like a **character** in the story: it comes, it stands, it runs swiftly, it does things. It is a way of talking about **God in action**, without separating Him from His speech.

Our English word **"word"** can sound small, like a single syllable. In the Old Testament, God's dābār is more like His **powerful, effective message and presence**.

2. Wisdom as God's partner in creation and guide for life

Alongside "word," the Old Testament and related books talk about **Wisdom** as if she were almost a person.

2.1. Wisdom in Proverbs

In Proverbs, especially chapter 8, **Wisdom** is personified as a woman who:

- Calls out in the streets.

- Was present "before the world began."

- Stood beside God when He created.

She is not a second god. Scholars describe her as a **poetic picture** of God's wise action:

- **Creative** – involved in ordering the world.

- **Revelatory** – showing humans how to live well.

- **Salvific** – leading people away from destruction and into life.

2.2. Wisdom in Sirach and Wisdom of Solomon

In some of the books found in Catholic and Orthodox canons (like **Sirach** and **Wisdom of Solomon**), Wisdom is described even more richly:

- She comes from God's throne.

- She searches everything.

- She enters people's lives and communities.

- She is closely tied to **Torah**, God's law/instruction.

These books are not in every Christian canon, but they show how Jewish thinkers were wrestling with the idea of **God's own wisdom** as an active, almost person-like presence.

2.3. Word and Wisdom together

Scholars have noticed that **Word** and **Wisdom** in these writings often do similar things:

- Both are linked to **creation**.

- Both **reveal** God's ways.

- Both are involved in **saving** and **guiding**.

They are ways of talking about **God reaching into the world**—without yet saying "God became human."

Our English word **"wisdom"** can sound like mere "good advice." In the Bible, God's Wisdom is much more: it is His **good order**, His **guidance**, and His **life-giving presence** at work.

3. Immanuel: "God with us" in Isaiah and Matthew

The name **Immanuel** appears first in the book of Isaiah. The prophet tells King Ahaz that a child will be born and called **Immanuel**, which means **"God with us."**

3.1. Immanuel in Isaiah's own time

In its original setting, Isaiah's prophecy is a **sign** to Ahaz:

- Enemies threaten Judah.

- God offers a sign that He is with His people.

- A child called Immanuel—"God with us"—will be a living reminder that God has not abandoned them.

Scholars have offered different views on who this child first referred to (possibly a royal child in Ahaz's court, or a prophetic sign-child). What matters for our purposes is that:

- The name Immanuel expresses a **promise**: God is present.

- Isaiah later uses the name again in a way that hints at a deeper fulfillment: the land is called "your land, O Immanuel," and the phrase "God is with us" is repeated.

Even in Isaiah, the name stretches beyond any one baby. It becomes a slogan of hope and warning: **"God is with us"—for rescue and for judgment.**

3.2. Immanuel in Matthew: God with us in a person

The Gospel of Matthew quotes Isaiah 7:14 and says:

"They shall call His name Immanuel," which means, "God with us."

Matthew sees in Jesus' birth the **fullest expression** of the Immanuel promise:

- Not just "God with us" in events or in history.

- Not just "God with us" as a comforting idea.

- But **God with us in a human life**.

Scholars who compare Isaiah and Matthew note that:

- Isaiah's Immanuel was a sign that God was involved in his people's crisis.

- Matthew's Immanuel is the **embodiment** of God's presence among His people.

Our English translations often leave **"Immanuel"** untranslated, then add "God with us" in a note or parenthesis. That can make the name feel like an exotic label. For Isaiah and Matthew, it is a **sentence**:

"God is with us."

4. "In the beginning was the Word": Logos in John's Gospel

With that Old Testament background—Word, Wisdom, and Immanuel in mind—we can come to the opening of John's Gospel:

"In the beginning was the Word (Logos), and the Word was with God, and the Word was God... And the Word became flesh and dwelt among us."

4.1. Logos: a familiar word with deep roots

In Greek, **logos** can simply mean:

* word,

* message, or

* reason/meaning.

Scholars note three main strands that feed John's use of **Logos**:

1. **Old Testament "word of the LORD"**

* In the Greek Old Testament, "word of the LORD" is often translated with **logos**.

* God's word creates, reveals, and acts.

1. **Personified Wisdom**

* Wisdom, in Proverbs and later writings, is God's wise power and presence, often described in personal terms.

* Some scholars see John's Logos as taking up that Wisdom imagery and applying it to Christ.

1. **Wider Jewish and Greek thought**

* Jewish thinkers like Philo talked about God's **Logos** as a way of speaking about His self-expression and ordering power.

* Greek philosophers used logos for the rational principle behind the universe.

John seems to **draw these strands together** in a uniquely Christian way: the Word that was with God and was God has now *become flesh*.

4.2. The Word that was with God and was God

John 1 says several staggering things about the Logos:

- The Word was **in the beginning**, echoing Genesis.

- The Word was **with God**, indicating distinction.

- The Word **was God**, indicating unity.

- Through the Word, **all things came into being**.

- The Word is also the source of **life** and **light**.

Scholars call this "Logos theology": a way of saying that **Jesus is God's self-expression, His creative and saving Word, now made human.**

Our English "Word" can sound like a static thing, like ink on a page. John's Logos is **God speaking and acting**, the same God who said "Let there be light," now stepping into the world in person.

4.3. "The Word became flesh and dwelt among us"

John then says:

"The Word became flesh and dwelt among us."

The phrase "dwelt among us" can also be translated "**tabernacled** among us," echoing the tent where God's presence once lived among Israel in the wilderness. Scholars see here an intentional link:

- The **tabernacle** and later the **temple** were places where God's presence was especially manifest.

- Now, God's Word—His Logos—has set up His **tent** in a human life.

This is where Word, Wisdom, and Immanuel meet:

- The **Word** that creates and reveals.

- The **Wisdom** that orders and saves.

- The **Immanuel** promise of "God with us."

All three themes converge in John's claim: **God's self-expression, His wisdom and word, has become a human being and lived among us.**

5. How "Word," "wisdom," and "Immanuel" get flattened in English

Our English words are accurate as far as they go, but they can flatten things if we're not careful.

5.1. "Word" as just a sound or a text

When we hear "Word of God" or "the Word":

- We may think mainly of the **Bible as a book**.

- We may think of spoken syllables.

The Bible certainly calls Scripture God's word. But in many passages, "the word of the LORD" means **God Himself in action**, and in John 1, "the Word" means **Jesus Himself**.

If we reduce "Word" to "text," we miss that the **living person** of Jesus is the ultimate Word through whom God speaks.

5.2. "Wisdom" as advice, not presence

In everyday English, **wisdom** often means "good advice" or "life hacks." Biblical Wisdom is far more:

- She is pictured as present before creation.

- She calls people into a right relationship with God.

- In some writings, she comes to dwell among God's people.

If we treat Wisdom only as "tips for living," we flatten a rich way of talking about **God's wise, saving work** in the world.

5.3. "Immanuel" as a Christmas label

For many of us, "Immanuel" is a word we hear mostly at Christmas in songs and cards. It can sound like a religious decoration.

In the Bible, **Immanuel** is a **promise and a warning**:

- God is with us—for salvation and for holy confrontation.

- His presence is good news and also serious news.

Matthew's use of Immanuel for Jesus says: **God's presence has become personal.** If we think of Immanuel only as a seasonal nickname, we miss how radical that claim is.

6. What did it say first—and how can we hear it now?

If we listen across Scripture:

- **"Word of the LORD"** first meant **God speaking and acting** in history.

- **"Wisdom"** first meant **God's wise ordering and guiding presence**, often pictured as a woman calling people to life.

- **"Immanuel"** first meant **"God with us"** in crisis—a sign of His involvement.

The New Testament then says:

- That **Word** has become flesh in Jesus.

- That **Wisdom** is found in Him.

- That He is the true **Immanuel**, God with us in person.

For us, that means:

- When we read "Word," we can think not just of sentences, but of **God's living self-expression**.

- When we read "wisdom," we can think not just of tips, but of **God's deep, active order and guidance**.

- When we see "Immanuel," we can remember that **God's presence has a face and a name**.

Try it yourself

Here are a few ways to work with these ideas in your own reading:

1. **Trace "word of the LORD" in the Old Testament**

- Pick a prophet (like Jeremiah or Amos).

- Underline "the word of the LORD came…" each time it appears.

- Ask: What does God's word **do** in this book—speak, warn, comfort, create hope?

1. **Read a Wisdom passage and John 1 side by side**

- Read Proverbs 8, imagining Wisdom speaking.

- Then read John 1:1–18.

- Note similarities: presence at creation, giving life, calling people to receive.

1. **Connect Immanuel in Isaiah and Matthew**

- Read Isaiah 7 and 8 to see how "Immanuel" works in its original context: "God with us" in the face of threats.

- Then read Matthew 1 and 28: "I am with you always."

- Ask: How does Jesus fulfill and deepen the Immanuel theme?

As you do this, "Word," "Wisdom," and "Immanuel" will start to sound less like thin religious terms and more like what they were from the beginning: powerful ways of saying that **the God who speaks, orders, and saves has come near in Jesus.**

Part III

What Is a Human Being?

Soul

Nephesh and Psychē

When many of us hear the word **"soul,"** we picture a ghost-like part inside us that can float away when we die. We imagine the "real me" as an invisible thing living inside a body. The Bible does use words that get translated "soul," but they do not start with that picture. In Hebrew and Greek, the main words behind our English "soul" are **nephesh** and **psychē**. Both are much more concrete and whole-person than we might expect.

This chapter asks: **What did nephesh and psychē say first?** How did they work in their own worlds, and how does our English word "soul" sometimes flatten them?

1. Nephesh in the Old Testament: a living, breathing person

The Hebrew noun **nephesh** ( )□□□□□□□shows up hundreds of times in the Old Testament. It is often translated "soul," but that English word only captures a slice of its meaning.

1.1. A breathing creature, a living life

Hebrew lexicons and word studies describe nephesh as:

- A **breathing creature**

- A **living being**

- **Life** itself

- A **person**

- The **self** or "I"

- Sometimes even a **dead body** in certain contexts

In other words, nephesh is not a small, invisible part of you. Nephesh is **you as a living, breathing being**. Scholars point out that the word is used not only for humans but also for animals:

- In Genesis 1, sea creatures and birds are called "living nephesh" (living creatures).

- In Genesis 2:7, when God forms the man from dust and breathes into his nostrils the breath of life, the man **becomes** a "living nephesh."

The man does not **receive** a nephesh; he **is** a nephesh—a living person animated by God's breath.

1.2. Nephesh as "life" and "self"

In many passages, nephesh clearly means **"life"** or "self":

- Someone can risk their nephesh, meaning they risk their **life**.

- Laws about punishment talk about taking a nephesh, meaning ending a life.

- A person can say "my nephesh" to mean **"me."**

Scholars note that translators render nephesh in various ways depending on context: "life," "soul," "person," "creature," "appetite," even "dead body."

The same Hebrew word lies under all those English terms.

1.3. Nephesh as the inner experience of a person

Nephesh can also speak of a person's **inner life**:

- A nephesh can be thirsty, downcast, joyful, or at rest.

- Psalms speak of nephesh thirsting for God, rejoicing, or waiting in silence.

This doesn't turn nephesh into a separate "spirit" floating inside a body. It shows that the **whole person**—the living nephesh—has desires, emotions, and thoughts. The Bible can talk about those inner experiences using the same word that also means "life" and "person."

1.4. Nephesh and death

In contexts of death, nephesh can refer to:

- A life that is departing ("her nephesh was departing, for she died").

- A dead nephesh in certain legal or ritual passages.

Scholars point out that this shows the **flexibility** of the word: it can speak of life, of a living person, of the inner self, and of a life that has ended. In all cases, the focus is on **the living being** in relation to God's breath, not on an abstract, detachable "soul" as in later philosophical systems.

2. Psychē in the New Testament: life, self, inner person

The main Greek word behind our English "soul" in the New Testament is **psychē** (ψυχή). It is the word that eventually gives us "psyche" in English (as in psychology). Like nephesh, it has a broad range of meanings.

2.1. Psychē in everyday Greek and in the Bible

In Greek, psychē can mean:

- **Life** (the fact that someone is alive)

- The **self** or "person"

- The **inner life** (thinking, feeling, choosing)

- In some contexts, the continuing **life of a person after death**

When Jewish translators rendered the Hebrew Bible into Greek, they often used **psychē** to translate **nephesh**. Many scholars note that this created a strong link: when New Testament writers use psychē, they inherit the **broad, concrete sense** of nephesh—life, self, whole person—while also functioning in a Greek world where people talk more sharply about "soul" and "body."

2.2. Psychē as "life"

In some of Jesus' sayings, psychē clearly means **life** in the ordinary sense:

- "Is not life (**psychē**) more than food?"

- "Whoever wants to save his psychē will lose it, but whoever loses his psychē for my sake will find it."

In English, these are often translated "life," not "soul," because the context clearly talks about **day-to-day life** and willingness to risk it, not about an invisible part.

2.3. Psychē as "self" and "inner person"

Psychē can also mean the **inner self**:

- Jesus says, "My psychē is very sorrowful," expressing deep inner anguish.

- Believers are told to love God with all their "heart, psychē, mind, and strength" (in some combinations), where psychē points to the **whole inner self**.

Here again, the focus is on the **person**—their thoughts, feelings, and choices.

2.4. Psychē and life beyond death

In some New Testament passages, psychē is used about **persons who have died**:

- Revelation speaks of the "psychai (souls)" of those who had been slain crying out to God.

- New Testament writers also draw on Old Testament language about God not abandoning "my nephesh" to the realm of the dead.

These uses show that the **person** continues in God's care even when the body has died, anticipating resurrection. Scholars caution, however, that we should not think of psychē as a completely separate, immortal "thing" in the way some Greek philosophers did. The Bible's hope centers on **resurrection of the whole person**, not just the survival of a disembodied "soul."

3. Nephesh and psychē together: an OT–NT bridge

Because Greek translators often used **psychē** to translate **nephesh**, the New Testament stands on a bridge between Hebrew and Greek ways of speaking.

3.1. Shared ground

On the **shared** side:

- Both nephesh and psychē can mean **life**.

- Both can mean **self** or "person."

- Both can speak of the **inner experience** of a living being.

- Both can be used in contexts of **danger, death, and hope**.

Scholarly comparisons of passages where Old Testament nephesh texts are quoted in Greek and then used in the New Testament (for example, Psalm 16:10 and Acts 2:27) show that psychē is often treated as the **equivalent** of nephesh. The basic idea of a **living person before God** carries through.

3.2. New Testament developments

The New Testament also lives in a world influenced by Greek thought, where people talk more sharply about "soul" and "body." Some passages reflect this more refined language:

- Certain texts speak of "spirit, soul, and body" as distinguishable aspects of a person.

- Psychē is sometimes used in ways that focus more on the **ongoing identity** of the person beyond death.

Scholars emphasize that even here, the New Testament does not deny the **Hebrew sense** of the whole person. Instead, it adds nuance: it can talk about different aspects (body, soul, spirit) without breaking the person into unrelated pieces.

4. How "soul" gets flattened in English

Our English word **"soul"** is not wrong, but it often carries extra baggage from later history:

- Many people think of the soul as a **tiny, ghost-like part** that lives inside the body and can float away.

- They imagine that the "real me" is that invisible soul, and the body is just a shell.

When we read "soul" in our Bibles with that picture already in our minds, we can flatten what nephesh and psychē were saying.

4.1. Shrinking the whole person

If nephesh and psychē usually mean **"whole living person,"** then translating them as "soul" can accidentally **shrink** the idea:

- Verses about risking your nephesh become, in English, about risking your "soul," as if they referred only to spiritual status instead of the **actual life** being put on the line.

- Commands to love God with all your nephesh can sound like "love God with your inner ghost," instead of "love God with all your life, your whole self."

Some Bible teachers have noted that in Hebrew, you do not "have" a nephesh; you **are** a nephesh. You are a living soul—meaning a living person. English often reverses that: we think we "have" souls rather than recognizing that we **are** souls in the biblical sense.

4.2. Over-spiritualizing Jesus' teaching

When Jesus talks about psychē, English translations sometimes say "soul," sometimes "life." That is already a clue that the word is broader than our usual idea of "soul."

If we always hear "soul" in a narrow, other-worldly way, we may:

- Read teachings about discipleship as if they only concern **life after death**, not whole-life allegiance now.

- Miss how Jesus talks about **losing** your life (psychē) for His sake in a very concrete, this-worldly sense.

A number of modern word studies warn about reading later philosophical meanings into biblical words. The safest path is to let the **contexts** tell us whether nephesh or psychē emphasizes life, person, inner self, or ongoing identity.

5. What did it say first—and how can we hear it now?

If we go back to the beginning:

- **Nephesh** first meant a **living, breathing creature**—a life, a person, a self.

- It then also came to express the **inner experiences** of that living self: desires, fears, joys.

- **Psychē**, picking up nephesh's range, also speaks of **life**, **self**, and **inner person**, with some added nuance in a Greek-speaking world.

So when we read "soul" in our English Bibles, we can train ourselves to ask:

- Does this passage mean **"life"**?

- Does it mean **"self"** or **"person"**?

- Does it focus on the **inner life** of a whole person?

- Is it speaking about the **ongoing identity** of the person before God, even through death?

Often, replacing "soul" in your mind with "life" or "self" will bring you closer to what nephesh or psychē meant to their first hearers.

This doesn't mean we deny that there is a part of us that can be in God's presence after death. It means we remember that the Bible's goal is **resurrected**

people in a renewed creation, not disembodied souls floating forever.

Try it yourself

Here are some simple exercises to help this chapter take root:

1. **Nephesh in creation**

- Read Genesis 1:20–21 and 2:7.

- Note where "living creatures" and "living being" appear.

- Remember that in Hebrew, these are "living nephesh."

- Ask: How does it change things to see humans and animals alike described this way?

1. **Nephesh in a psalm**

- Read Psalm 42 ("Why are you cast down, O my soul?").

- Try paraphrasing "my soul" as "my whole self," "my life," or "my inner being."

- Notice how the psalmist is not talking to a ghost but to his own **self**.

1. **Psychē in Jesus' teaching**

- Read one of Jesus' sayings about losing and finding your "life/soul" (for example, Mark 8:34–37).

- Check different translations to see where they choose "life" or "soul."

- Ask: What happens if I hear psychē here as "life" or "self" instead of only "immortal soul"?

As you practice, your picture of "soul" will slowly shift from a thin, floating thing to a thick, biblical idea: **the whole living person before God, with all their life and inner depths.**

Chapter 12

Spirit and Breath

Ruach and Pneuma

When you hear the word **"spirit,"** what do you picture? A ghostly shape? A vague feeling? In the Bible, the main words behind our English "spirit" are **ruach** in Hebrew and **pneuma** in Greek. Both literally mean **"breath"** or **"wind,"** and then, by extension, "spirit."

This chapter asks: **What did ruach and pneuma say first?** How did they work in their own worlds, and how does our English "spirit" sometimes flatten or distort them?

1. Ruach in the Old Testament: wind, breath, spirit

The Hebrew word **ruach** ( )□□□□□appears almost 400 times in the Old Testament. Scholars agree that it has a broad range of meanings, all related to **invisible but powerful movement**.

1.1. Ruach as wind

At the most basic level, ruach can mean **wind**:

- A wind sent by God to move waters or bring locusts.

- A powerful storm wind.

- The "four winds" of heaven.

In these contexts, translators use "wind," because the text is clearly talking about **moving air** in the natural world. Yet even here, the Old Testament often reminds readers that **God directs the wind**. Every gust is under His hand.

1.2. Ruach as breath

Ruach also means **breath**—the air flowing in and out of a living being:

- Job says that in God's hand is the life of every living thing and the **ruach** of all humankind.

- Passages speak of breath leaving a person when they die.

Ancient people did not separate "breath" and "spirit" as sharply as we often do. For them, breath **was** a sign of life, and life was tied to spirit. When someone stopped breathing, their "spirit" had gone.

1.3. Ruach as human spirit

Ruach can also refer to a person's **inner life** or "spirit":

- A person can have a broken ruach, a patient ruach, a proud ruach.

- Ruach can mean inner strength, mood, or disposition.

In these uses, ruach is not about lungs or weather; it is about the **invisible energy** and **inner attitude** that drive a person.

1.4. Ruach as God's Spirit

Finally, ruach refers to **God's own Spirit**:

- In Genesis 1:2, the ruach of God hovers over the waters.

- God's ruach gives life, empowers leaders, inspires prophets, and renews creation.

- Some texts speak of the "Spirit of the LORD" or "the Holy Spirit."

Scholars warn that context is crucial: sometimes ruach means ordinary wind, sometimes breath, sometimes human spirit, sometimes **the** Spirit of God. The same word stretches across all these uses, but it always points to something **invisible, powerful, and life-related**.

2. Pneuma in the New Testament: wind, breath, spirit

The main Greek word behind our English "spirit" is **pneuma** (πνεῦμα). Like ruach, it can mean **wind, breath, or spirit**.

2.1. Pneuma as wind and breath

In Greek literature and in the New Testament, pneuma can describe:

- A movement of air—a **wind**.

- **Breath** from the mouth or nostrils.

For example, in John 3, Jesus uses the same word for **wind** and **Spirit**:

- "The wind (pneuma) blows where it wishes... so it is with everyone born of the Spirit (pneuma)."

In some translations, this double use is hidden (wind / Spirit), but in Greek it is **one word**, playing on the overlap.

2.2. Pneuma as human spirit

Pneuma also refers to a person's **spirit**:

- The inner part of a person that can be joyful, troubled, or willing.

- The aspect that relates to God in a special way.

In some passages, writers distinguish between **spirit, soul, and body** to talk about different aspects of the person. Scholars point out that these are **aspects**, not separate little "things" inside us. They describe the whole person from different angles.

2.3. Pneuma as God's Spirit and other spirits

Most importantly, pneuma refers to **the Holy Spirit**:

- The Spirit who descends on Jesus at His baptism.

- The Spirit who fills and leads believers.

- The Spirit who speaks through prophets and apostles.

Pneuma can also refer to **other spirits**:

- Good spirits (angels).

- Evil spirits (demons).

- "Unclean spirits" in the Gospels.

Lexicons summarize pneuma's range as: wind, breath, human spirit, spirit beings, and God's Spirit. Once again, context matters.

3. Ruach and pneuma together: a shared picture

Because the Greek Old Testament often uses **pneuma** to translate **ruach**, the New Testament inherits the Old Testament's rich picture.

3.1. Shared core ideas

Across both Testaments, ruach/pneuma carries a cluster of ideas:

- **Invisible movement** – like wind that you can't see but can feel.

- **Breath and life** – the presence or absence of breath signals life or death.

- **Inner energy** – the "spirit" of a person, their courage, mood, or resolve.

- **Divine presence and power** – God's own Spirit moving in creation, revelation, and salvation.

Scholars often emphasize that ancient people did not see "breath" and "spirit" as separate things. Breath was the **sign** of spirit. When a person breathed, they were animated by a ruach/pneuma. When they stopped breathing, their spirit had gone.

3.2. Old Testament roots of New Testament pneuma

When the New Testament speaks of:

- The **Spirit of God** hovering,

- People being "filled with the Holy Spirit,"

- The Spirit giving life,

- The Spirit as a down payment of future resurrection,

it is building on Old Testament texts where ruach:

- Gives life to dry bones.

- Comes on judges and kings.

- Shapes creation and renews the earth.

Scholarly surveys of ruach and pneuma across Scripture show that the **same basic picture** (breath/wind/spirit) supports both Old and New Testament uses. The New Testament develops doctrine about the Holy Spirit, but it does not abandon the old imagery.

4. How "spirit" gets flattened or confused in English

Our English word **"spirit"** is narrower than ruach/pneuma in some ways and fuzzier in others.

4.1. Losing the "wind/breath" side

When we read "Spirit," we often:

- Think of a **vague, invisible something**.

- Forget the concrete link to **wind and breath**.

This can make Bible passages feel more abstract than they were:

- The Spirit hovering over the waters was not a misty idea but God's **moving, life-giving presence**.

- The Spirit giving life to dry bones in Ezekiel's vision is pictured as **breath/wind** entering bodies.

If we keep the breath/wind connection in mind, "Spirit" becomes more tangible and powerful.

4.2. Mixing up "spirit" and "soul"

In everyday English, people sometimes use "spirit" and "soul" interchangeably. In the Bible, ruach/pneuma and nephesh/psychē overlap but are not identical:

- **Nephesh/psychē** emphasizes the **whole living person**, life, and self.

- **Ruach/pneuma** emphasizes **breath, inner energy, and God's presence**.

If we blur them, we can:

- Treat "spirit" as just another word for "soul,"

- Lose the specific imagery of **breath and wind** that is so important for understanding the Holy Spirit.

Scholars studying these words often stress the need to keep their **distinct flavors** clear, even though they work together in describing a human being.

4.3. Treating the Holy Spirit as an "it"

Because "spirit" can sound like an impersonal force, some readers think of the Holy Spirit as an "it":

- A kind of energy.

- A feeling.

- A vague presence.

The New Testament, however, speaks of the Holy Spirit in **personal** terms:

- He speaks, teaches, guides, can be grieved, resisted, lied to.

- He gives gifts, leads the church, and glorifies Christ.

When "Spirit" is heard only as "force," we flatten the biblical picture of the Holy Spirit as **God's personal presence and power**.

5. What did it say first—and how can we hear it now?

If we go back to the roots:

- **Ruach** first said **wind**—moving air under God's control.

- It then said **breath**, the sign of life.

- It then said **spirit**—the inner drive of a person.

- It finally said **Spirit**—God's own powerful, life-giving presence.

Pneuma follows the same path in Greek:

- Wind, breath, spirit, Spirit.

So when you see "spirit" or "Spirit" in your English Bible, you can ask:

- Is this talking about **wind**?

- Is it about **breath** or **life**?

- Is it about a **person's inner spirit**—their attitude, courage, or mood?

- Is it about **God's own Spirit**, His active presence?

Often, remembering the **wind/breath** side will give you a clearer, richer sense of the verse.

For example:

- "The Spirit gives life" can also be heard as "God's **breath** gives life."

- "Be filled with the Spirit" can be imagined as "let God's **living breath** fill and move you."

- "Born of the Spirit" can be pictured with Jesus' wind analogy: a new **breath of life** from God.

Try it yourself

Here are a few ways to practice hearing ruach and pneuma more clearly:

1. **Ruach in creation and new creation**

- Read Genesis 1:2 and Ezekiel 37:1–14.

- Note how ruach appears as **God's Spirit**, as **wind**, and as **breath** in the dry bones vision.

- Ask: How does the breath/wind imagery help me understand what God is doing?

1. **Pneuma in John 3**

- Read John 3:5–8, noting where English says "wind" and where it says "Spirit."

- Remember that in Greek, both are **pneuma**.

- Ask: What does Jesus' comparison between wind and Spirit teach about new birth?

1. **Human spirit vs Holy Spirit**

- Find one passage where "spirit" clearly refers to a **person's inner life** (for example, someone's spirit being troubled).

- Find another where "Spirit" clearly refers to **the Holy Spirit**.

- Notice the similarities (invisible, inner, moving) and the differences (human vs divine).

As you practice, "spirit" will begin to sound less like a vague religious word and more like what it was at first: **breath, wind, and the powerful, invisible life of God at work in and around us.**

Chapter 13

Flesh and Body

Basar, Sarx, and Sōma

When many of us read **"flesh"** and **"body"** in our English Bibles, we hear them through a split lens: "flesh" sounds dirty or evil, and "body" sounds like a shell for the "real" inner person. In Scripture, the main words behind our English terms are **basar** in Hebrew and **sarx** and **sōma** in Greek. They do not start with a simple "body bad, spirit good" idea.

This chapter asks: **What did basar, sarx, and sōma say first?** How did they describe human life, weakness, and dignity, and how does English sometimes flatten them into a body-vs-soul battle God never intended?

1. Basar in the Old Testament: flesh, body, kin, humanity

The Hebrew word **bāśār** ( )□□□□□□□□literally means **"flesh"**—the soft tissue of humans and animals. From that basic picture, its meaning widens.

1.1. Flesh as the soft, living stuff

Lexicons describe basar as:

- The **flesh** that covers bones and is filled with blood.

- The **meat** of animals and humans.

- The **body** itself in contrast to bones.

In many passages, it simply refers to physical flesh:

- A wound in the flesh.

- Flesh that is healthy or diseased.

- Flesh as food.

In this sense, basar is very concrete. It is the **material aspect** of living beings.

1.2. Flesh as the whole person and kinship

From that literal meaning, basar also comes to mean:

- The **body** as a whole.

- A **person** (because a person has flesh).

- **Kinship**, as in "You are my bone and my flesh," meaning "You are my own family."

Statements like "we are your bone and flesh" are ways of saying, "We belong together." Basar becomes a way to speak of **family bonds** and **solidarity**.

1.3. Flesh as all humanity and frailty

Prophets and poets also use basar to mean **all living creatures** or **all humanity**:

- "All flesh will see the glory of the LORD."

- "All flesh is grass," highlighting **weakness and mortality**.

Here, "flesh" means "all living humans (and sometimes animals) in their **fragility**." It is not a moral insult; it is a reminder that we are **limited, temporary, and dependent**.

So in the Old Testament, basar can be:

- Flesh as physical tissue.

- Flesh as **body** and **person**.

- Flesh as **family**.

- Flesh as **all living creatures** in their frailty.

2. Sarx and Sōma in the New Testament: flesh and body

The New Testament mainly uses two Greek words where English has "flesh" and "body": **sarx** (σάρξ) and **sōma** (σῶμα).

2.1. Sarx: flesh in several senses

In ordinary Greek, **sarx** means **flesh**—the soft tissue covering bones, the meat of animals, the vulnerable part of living beings. New Testament lexicons and word studies show sarx being used in several ways:

1. **Literal flesh / physical body**

- The flesh of humans or animals.

- Circumcision "in the flesh."

- "All flesh" meaning all living creatures.

1. **Human weakness and mortality**

- People described as "in the flesh" to highlight their frailty and earthly life.

- "Flesh" contrasted with God's Spirit.

1. **The "sphere" of fallen human nature**

- In Paul's letters, "flesh" (sarx) sometimes describes the **realm of life turned away from God**—the pattern of desires and behavior that resists the Spirit.

This third use is the one many people know: "walking according to the flesh," "the works of the flesh," and so on. It does not mean the body itself is evil. It means **human life dominated by self-centered desires and opposed to God**.

Careful studies of sarx in Paul stress:

- Sarx is sometimes neutral (just "flesh/body").

- Sometimes it is a shorthand for **human weakness**.

- Sometimes it names a **powerful pattern** of life opposed to the Spirit.

Context tells you which is in play.

2.2. Sōma: body as whole person and corporate body

The Greek word **sōma** is usually translated **"body."** It can mean:

- The physical **body** of a person or animal.

- A **corpse**.

- The **whole person**, especially in relation to others and to God.

- A **group** viewed as one body (like the church as the body of Christ).

When Paul says the church is the **body (sōma) of Christ**, he is using "body" as an image of:

- Unity in diversity (many parts, one body).

- Connection to Christ (He is the head, we are the members).

- Concrete, visible life together.

Sōma, especially in Paul, is not just "material stuff." It is the **person in community**, the person as present and active in the world. Scholars on sōma emphasize that the biblical view of "body" is **relational and personal**, not merely physical.

3. Flesh, body, and "flesh vs Spirit" in Paul

Many misunderstandings of "flesh" come from a quick reading of Paul's letters. Some conclude:

- Flesh = physical body = bad.

- Spirit = non-physical part = good.

That is not what Paul actually says.

3.1. Flesh as a "realm" or pattern of life

When Paul uses sarx in a negative sense, he often contrasts it with **Spirit**:

- "Those who live according to the flesh set their minds on the things of the flesh, but those according to the Spirit on the things of the Spirit."

- "The works of the flesh" vs "the fruit of the Spirit."

Here, "flesh" means:

- The **old way of being human**, centered on self, closed to God.

- The **sphere** in which sin operates.

- A life **dominated** by disordered desires.

Many scholars describe this as "flesh" as a **realm** or "mode" of existence, not as the physical body itself. Your body is not the enemy; it is the place where either the **flesh** or the **Spirit** can be in charge.

3.2. Body as honored, destined for resurrection

Paul also speaks highly of the **body (sōma)**:

- He calls the body a **temple** of the Holy Spirit.

- He speaks of offering our bodies as a **living sacrifice**.

- He insists on the **resurrection of the body**, not just the survival of a soul.

In 1 Corinthians 15, he talks about a **spiritual body**, not a body-less spirit. "Spiritual" there means "from the Spirit," not "made of spirit stuff." The **body matters**; it will be transformed, not discarded.

So:

- Paul can criticize "flesh" in the moral/spiritual sense while affirming the goodness and future of the **body**.

- A careful reading shows that the problem is not having a body, but being **ruled by fleshly desires** instead of by God's Spirit.

4. How "flesh" and "body" get flattened today

Our English words can flatten this picture if we're not careful.

4.1. Treating the body as the problem

When we hear "flesh" and read it as "body," we may:

- See the body as anti-spiritual.

- Think that holiness means **escaping** the body.

- Confuse Christian hope (resurrection) with some non-Christian ideas (leaving the body behind forever).

This leads to a body-vs-soul split that can:

- Devalue **physical health** and embodied life.

- Make us ignore physical needs in favor of only "spiritual" ministry.

- Create shame around normal bodily experiences.

The Bible's actual picture is more integrated: we are **embodied souls** (or ensouled bodies), and God cares for us as whole persons.

4.2. Ignoring "flesh" as a pattern, not just a thing

If we only think of "flesh" as physical, we may miss how Paul uses it as a shorthand for a **way of living**:

- The works of the flesh (envy, strife, sexual immorality, etc.) are not just "body things"; they are **whole-person patterns** of life without God.

- Walking "according to the flesh" describes people who rely on their own strength, status, or desires instead of on God.

If we reduce "flesh" to "body," we might focus on only one area (like sexual sin) and ignore deeper issues (like pride, greed, or hatred).

4.3. Missing the corporate "body"

When we hear "body of Christ," we might think only of:

- A metaphor for unity, or

- A spiritual idea, not concrete relationships.

In Scripture, the **sōma of Christ** is:

- A **real community** of people.

- A **visible, local gathering** and a worldwide reality.

- A picture of Christ's presence in the world.

If we flatten "body" into a vague idea, we may miss how seriously the New Testament takes our **embodied life together**—serving, suffering, rejoicing as one.

5. What did it say first—and how can we hear it now?

If we listen carefully:

- **Basar** first said **flesh**—soft tissue—then grew to mean **body, person, kin, and all humanity** in its weakness.

- **Sarx** first said **flesh**—the soft stuff—then came to include **human weakness** and, in some contexts, **the realm of life opposed to the Spirit**.

- **Sōma** said **body**, then also **whole person** and **corporate body** (especially the church).

For us, that means:

- When we see "flesh," we should ask: Is this about **physical tissue, human frailty**, or the **old way of living without God**?

- When we see "body," we should ask: Is this about the **physical organism**, the **whole person offered to God**, or the **community** that is Christ's body?

Holding those questions in mind helps us avoid both extremes:

- Seeing the body as bad, or

- Ignoring the real struggle between **fleshly patterns** and **Spirit-led life**.

The Bible's vision is that God created our bodies good, that sin has twisted how we live in them, and that the Spirit is at work to **renew us as whole embodied people**, both now and in the resurrection.

Try it yourself

Here are a few exercises to help this chapter come alive:

1. **Basar and "all flesh"**

- Read Isaiah 40:5–8, noting the phrase "all flesh is grass."

- Paraphrase "all flesh" as "all human beings in their weakness."

- Ask: How does that affect the way I hear the contrast with God's enduring word?

1. **Sarx and "flesh" in Paul**

- Read Galatians 5:16–25.

- List the "works of the flesh" and the "fruit of the Spirit."

- Notice how many "works of the flesh" are not about the body as such but about **relational and inner attitudes**.

1. **Sōma as body and church**

- Read 1 Corinthians 12:12–27 and Ephesians 4:11–16.

- Underline every occurrence of "body."

- Ask: What does it mean for my local church to be **Christ's body** in this concrete, relational sense?

As you practice, "flesh" and "body" will move from being flat, negative or purely physical terms to what they were from the beginning: words that describe our **real, fragile, embodied lives** and the way God is redeeming them.

Chapter 14

Heart

Lev and Kardia

In many modern cultures, the **heart** is the place of feelings. "Follow your heart" means "follow your emotions." In the Bible, the words we translate "heart" are **lev** (or levav) in Hebrew and **kardia** in Greek. They include emotions, but they are much bigger: the **inner center** of thought, will, desire, and conscience.

This chapter asks: **What did "heart" say first?** How does it work in Scripture, and how does our narrow, feelings-only idea of "heart" flatten it?

1. Lev in the Old Testament: the inner center

The Hebrew **lev / levav** ( )□□□□□ / □□□literally names the physical heart, but most of the time it refers to the **inner person**.

1.1. Heart as mind and thoughts

In Hebrew, people **think** with their hearts:

- "As a man thinks in his heart, so is he."

- God tests and knows the thoughts of the heart.

Scholars note that there is no separate everyday word for "brain" in biblical Hebrew. The **lev** is the seat of **thinking, reflecting, planning, and understanding.**

1.2. Heart as will and decisions

The heart is also where people **choose**:

- Hearts can be hard or soft toward God.

- People "set their heart" to seek the LORD.

- God's commands are written on the heart.

Word studies show lev used for **intentions**, **plans**, and **moral choices**—the **steering wheel** of a person's life.

1.3. Heart as emotions and conscience

Lev includes **feelings** as well:

- Hearts rejoice, tremble, grieve, melt, grow proud, or are struck with guilt.

- David's heart "struck him" after he sinned, a way of describing **conscience** waking up.

So in the Old Testament, **lev** is:

- Your **mind** (what you think).

- Your **will** (what you decide).

- Your **desires and emotions** (what you love, fear, hate).

- Your **conscience** (what accuses or comforts you).

When God says, "Love the LORD your God with all your heart," He is not asking only for warm feelings. He is asking for your **whole inner self**—thoughts, choices, desires, and moral center.

2. Kardia in the New Testament: the inner life continued

The Greek word **kardia** (καρδία) gives us the English "cardiac." Like lev, it can mean the physical organ, but its main biblical use is **figurative**.

2.1. Kardia as the seat of thought and understanding

New Testament writers inherit the Hebrew idea:

- Jesus knows the **thoughts** in people's hearts.

- Paul prays that the "eyes of your heart" may be enlightened.

Lexical studies summarize kardia as the **center of thinking, understanding, and reasoning**, not just feeling.

2.2. Kardia as desire, emotion, and will

Kardia is also where people:

- Desire and lust.

- Grieve and rejoice.

- Decide and intend.

Scholars describe it as the **inner control center** where desires and decisions meet.

2.3. Kardia as the place of faith and renewal

Crucially, kardia is where **faith** happens:

- "With the **heart** one believes and is justified."

- The Lord opens Lydia's heart to respond.

- God promises a **new heart** in fulfillment of Old Testament hopes.

Studies of kardia note that it "gathers the whole interior life—thinking, feeling, choosing—into a single term" that God searches, renews, and indwells by His Spirit.

3. Heart in Scripture: more than feelings

When we put lev and kardia together, a clear picture emerges.

- The **heart** is the **unified inner center** of a person:

- Thoughts

- Desires

- Emotions

- Choices

- Conscience

- The heart directs **everything else**: "Above all else, guard your heart, for from it flow the springs of life."

Because of this:

- Sin is rooted in the **heart** (idolatry, hardness, deceit).

- Obedience and love begin in the **heart**.

- God's promise of a new covenant focuses on a **new heart**—His law written there, His Spirit changing it from the inside out.

In modern English, we often reduce "heart" to **emotion**—especially romantic feeling. The Bible's heart includes emotion but is much larger. It is closer to what we would call the **inner self** or **identity**—mind, will, desires, and feelings together.

4. How "heart" gets flattened today

Our English use of "heart" can flatten the biblical idea in a few ways.

4.1. Heart as only feelings

If we hear "heart" as only emotions:

- "Love God with all your heart" becomes "feel warmly about God," rather than "devote your whole **inner life** to Him."

- "Guard your heart" becomes "guard your feelings," rather than "guard what shapes your **thinking, desires, and choices**."

- This can lead us to chase certain **experiences** (feeling close to God) and neglect deeper habits of mind and will (learning His ways, obeying when we don't feel like it).

4.2. Splitting "heart" from "mind"

Because we say "head vs heart," we may imagine:

- Mind = logic.

- Heart = feelings.

In Scripture, the **heart thinks**. It understands, plans, and reasons. When Jesus and Paul talk about the heart, they do not place it in opposition to the mind; they treat it as the **core of our thinking and choosing.**

If we split them, we might try to serve God with "head knowledge" only or chase "heart experiences" only, instead of offering God our **whole inner self**.

4.3. Treating "heart change" as vague

"Change of heart" can sound like a soft metaphor for "slightly different feelings." Biblically, a **new heart** is a deep, comprehensive change:

- New ways of thinking and valuing.

- New desires.

- New choices and habits.

- A new inner orientation toward God.

New Testament studies on kardia stress that when God gives a new heart, He is remaking the **entire inner person**, not tweaking mood.

5. What did it say first—and how can we hear it now?

If we go back to the roots:

- **Lev** in the Old Testament is the **center of human thought, desire, decision, and emotion**—the inner person God sees and addresses.

- **Kardia** in the New Testament carries that same meaning: the **whole interior life** that must be transformed by grace.

So when we read "heart" in our English Bibles, we can train ourselves to think:

- Not just "feelings," but **my whole inner self**.

- Not just "romantic heart," but **what I think, want, love, choose, and believe**.

- Not just "emotional warmth," but **deep, directional loyalty**.

That means:

- Loving God with all your heart = loving Him with your **thoughts, desires, plans, and emotions**.

- Guarding your heart = being careful what shapes your **thinking and wanting**.

- Asking God for a clean heart = asking Him to **rebuild you from the inside out**.

Try it yourself

Here are a few ways to work with "heart" as the Bible uses it:

1. **Read the Shema with "heart" expanded**

- Read Deuteronomy 6:5.

- Paraphrase "heart" as "inner self—mind, will, and desires."

- Pray it back to God that way.

1. **Track "heart" in a psalm**

- Choose a psalm that mentions "heart" (for example, Psalm 51).

- Every time you see "heart," mentally substitute "my inner life" or "my true self."

- Notice how comprehensive David's plea really is.

1. **Heart and faith in the New Testament**

- Read Romans 10:9–10 and Acts 16:14.

- Ask: What does it mean that belief happens "with the heart," and that God "opened" Lydia's heart?

- Consider how this involves understanding, trust, and willingness—not just a feeling.

As you practice, "heart" will begin to sound less like a narrow emotional word and more like what it was from the beginning: the **deep center** of who you are, where God wants to write His law, pour out His love, and from which your whole life flows.

Chapter 15

Humanity and the Image of God

Adam and Anthrōpos

The Bible does not begin with isolated souls or disembodied spirits. It begins with a **human**—adam, "earthling," formed from dust and filled with breath—and with a declaration that this human creature, male and female, is made **"in the image of God."** The Greek New Testament then speaks of the **anthrōpos**, the human being, and calls Jesus the "last Adam," the true human who restores what was lost. This chapter asks: **What did "Adam," "image," and "anthrōpos" say first?** And how can hearing them rightly reshape how we see ourselves and our neighbors?

1. Adam: dust, breath, and every human

In Hebrew, the word **'adam** can refer to:

- A particular man (Adam in Genesis 2–4).

- "The human" in a collective sense.

- "Humankind" in general.

The connection between 'adam and **'adamah** ("ground" or "soil") is deliberate. Genesis 2 pictures God forming the human from the dust of the ground and breathing into his nostrils the breath of life so that he becomes a **living soul**—a living person, dust and breath together. The first human is earthling and God-breathed at once.

As the story unfolds, 'adam can name the individual "Adam" and also stand for **humanity as a whole**. When Genesis says, "God created the 'adam in his image," and "male and female he created them," it signals that **being human, male and female together**, is tied to this image.

2. "In our image, after our likeness": what image meant first

Genesis 1:26–27 is brief but dense:

- Humans are made in God's **image** (tselem) and **likeness** (demuth).

- They are given a royal-sounding task: to **rule** over other creatures.

- Male and female together bear this image.

In the ancient Near Eastern world, an "image" of a god was often a **statue** placed in a temple or territory to represent the deity's presence and authority. By calling humans God's image, Genesis draws on that background but transforms it:

- The **whole human race** is God's living image, not just kings.

- The **world itself** becomes God's temple.

- To be God's image is to be His **representative**—to reflect His character and exercise delegated rule in His world.

The image is not a small "part" of us, like a soul hidden inside. It is a **vocation** and a **status**: we are made to mirror God's character and to steward creation under His authority.

3. Male and female: the image as a shared calling

Genesis is careful to say:

"In the image of God he created him; male and female he created them."

This means:

- The image is borne by **both sexes together**.

- There is no hint that one sex is closer to God's image than the other.

- Humanity's task—to be fruitful, to fill the earth, to rule and cultivate—requires **male and female together**.

The image of God, then, is **relational** as well as royal. Humans image God as they live **with** each other and **before** Him, reflecting His relational, faithful character in their own relationships and responsibilities.

4. Anthrōpos in the New Testament: the human being

The Greek word **anthrōpos** simply means **"human being."** It can be translated "man" in older English, but it usually means "person" or "human," not specifically "male." In the New Testament, anthrōpos is used:

- For individual persons (a man, a woman, someone).

- For humanity in general ("the inner human," "the old human," "the new human").

- In theological contrasts between Adam and Christ.

When Paul speaks of "the old anthrōpos" and "the new anthrōpos," he is talking about **old and new humanity**, old and new ways of being human, not about some inner "ghost person" detached from the body. Anthrōpos is the human creature in full.

5. Adam and Christ: old humanity and new humanity

The New Testament draws a direct line from **Adam** to **Christ**:

- Adam is "the first human," through whom sin and death enter the human story.

- Christ is "the last Adam" or "second human," through whom resurrection and new life come.

This comparison does two things:

1. It treats Adam not only as an individual but as a kind of **head** or representative of the human family.

2. It presents Jesus as the **true human**, the one who images God fully and faithfully, and who starts a **new humanity** in Himself.

Where Adam fails in vocation—failing to trust, obey, and reflect God's character—Jesus succeeds. Where Adam's disobedience pulls humanity into sin and death, Jesus' obedience opens the way for humans to be remade in God's image.

6. Image and likeness after the fall

After Genesis 3, humans continue to be spoken of as **in God's image**:

- Murder is condemned because the victim is made in God's image.

- Humans, even in their brokenness, retain a kind of **echo** of that original status and calling.

Yet the New Testament also speaks of the image as something that must be **renewed**:

- Believers are being **conformed to the image of Christ**.

- The "new human" is being renewed in **knowledge after the image of its Creator**.

This suggests that:

- The image of God is **not lost** by sin, but it is **damaged, obscured, and distorted**.

- Jesus, as the perfect image of God, restores and renews that image in those who belong to Him.

In other words, the image is both **given** (by creation) and **being restored** (by redemption).

7. What this means for how we see people

If every human being is an **adam**—dust and breath, bearing God's image—and if Jesus is the **anthrōpos** who renews humanity, several implications follow.

1. **Dignity**

- Every person, regardless of age, sex, ability, ethnicity, or status, bears the image of God.

- This grounds human worth not in productivity, feeling, or social standing, but in God's creative decision.

1. **Responsibility**

- As God's image, humans are entrusted with **stewardship** over creation and care for one another.

- Our treatment of the earth and of our neighbors is part of our imaging of God—for good or ill.

1. **Humility**

- We are made from dust; we are not gods.

- Our breath is borrowed; our life is dependent.

1. **Hope**

- The image, though marred, is being restored.

- In Christ, humans can begin to live as **new humanity**, reflecting God's character more truly even now, and awaiting a final renewal in resurrection.

8. How our language can flatten "humanity" and "image"

Modern talk about "being human" and "the image of God" can flatten these ideas.

- "Human" can be used as an excuse for sin ("I'm only human"), rather than a calling to **bear God's likeness**.

- "Image of God" can be vague—reduced to "we can think" or "we have souls"—instead of a rich calling to **represent God's rule and character** in the world.

- "Humanity" can be abstract, forgetting that in Scripture it is always **embodied and communal**: male and female, families and peoples, in real places and histories.

Returning to **adam** and **anthrōpos** reminds us that to be human is to be **placed** (in a world), **tasked** (to cultivate and care), **related** (to God and others), and **summoned** (to reflect the Creator).

9. What did it say first—and how can we hear it now?

If we listen to these words in their own setting:

- **Adam / 'adam** says: **earthling**, human formed from dust, animated by God's breath, made in God's image to represent Him in the world.

- **Image and likeness** say: royal representative, living statue, called to mirror God's character and rule.

- **Anthrōpos** says: the **human being**, individually and collectively, old humanity in Adam and new humanity in Christ.

For us, hearing them this way can:

- Deepen our sense of **human dignity and responsibility**.

- Clarify that salvation is not escape from being human, but the **renewal of our humanity** in Christ.

- Teach us to see every neighbor as a fellow image-bearer, every Christian as part of a new humanity, and our own bodies and lives as places where God's image is meant to shine.

Try it yourself

Here are a few ways to work with these ideas:

1. **Read Genesis 1–2 with "image" in mind**

- Mark every mention of God's image, human rule, and God's blessing.

- Ask: What kind of **role** is being described for humans?

1. **Trace Adam and Christ in one of Paul's letters**

- Read Romans 5 or 1 Corinthians 15 and underline "Adam," "man," and "image" language.

- Note how Paul contrasts **old humanity in Adam** with **new humanity in Christ**.

1. **Practice seeing people as image-bearers**

- Choose one ordinary setting (work, school, a store) and quietly remind yourself: "Every person I see is an image-bearer, dust and breath, loved and summoned by God."

- Notice how that changes your reactions and choices.

As you do this, "human," "image," "Adam," and "anthrōpos" will move from being abstract religious terms to what they were at the beginning: living words that tell you **who you are, whose you are, and what you are for**.

Chapter 16

God's People Gathered

Qahal and Ekklesia

The Bible's story is not just about God and individual souls. It is about **God and a people**. From the first assembly at Sinai to the gatherings of the early Christians, God calls people **together**—to hear His word, to share His life, and to bear His name in the world. The Old Testament word for this gathered people is often **qahal**. The New Testament word most often translated "church" is **ekklesia**. Both point, first of all, not to buildings, programs, or institutions, but to **people assembled** because God has summoned them.

This chapter asks: **What did qahal and ekklesia say first?** How did they shape Israel's and the church's self-understanding, and how can hearing them rightly reshape how we think about "church" today?

1. Qahal in the Old Testament: the summoned assembly

The Hebrew root **qahal** (verb) means **"to assemble, to gather"**, and the noun **qahal** means **"assembly, congregation, gathering."** It describes a **people called together for a purpose**, not a casual crowd.

1.1. A gathered people under God's word

In key passages, qahal describes **Israel gathered**:

- At Sinai, to hear God's covenant words.

- For festivals and feasts in Jerusalem.

- For covenant renewal ceremonies.

- For important decisions or warfare under recognized leaders.

This is not just "whoever happens to be around." It is a people **summoned**—by God, through Moses or other leaders—to gather, listen, respond, and act together. Worship is not merely private devotion; it is a **public assembly** around God's presence and word.

1.2. Assembly for worship, war, and justice

Qahal shows up in **religious, political, and military** contexts:

- The assembly gathers for **worship** and sacrifice.

- The assembly gathers to **consult** or to judge.

- The assembly gathers for **battle**, acting as one under God's direction.

This breadth matters. Israel is not just a religious crowd that meets once a week. It is a **whole people**, whose life—worship, justice, and even warfare—is lived as a gathered community under God. Qahal is a reminder that God's people are called to act **together**.

1.3. Misused and promised assemblies

The Old Testament also shows qahal being **misused**:

- People assemble to demand an idol.

- Crowds gather against God's prophets.

At the same time, the prophets speak of God's promise to **re-gather** His scattered people, reversing exile. The root idea of qahal becomes part of a forward-looking hope: God will one day assemble a **purified community**, even from among the nations, under His king.

2. Ekklesia in the New Testament: the called-out assembly

The Greek word **ekklesia** is built from **ek** ("out/from") and **kaleō** ("to call"). Literally, it suggests a **"called-out assembly."** In everyday Greek before the New Testament, it referred to:

- A **public meeting** of citizens called out for civic business.

- Any kind of assembly—political, social, sometimes even riotous.

It did not start as a religious technical term; it was a common word for a **gathering of people called together**.

2.1. Ekklesia in the Greek Old Testament

When Jewish translators rendered the Hebrew Bible into Greek (the Septuagint), they often used **ekklesia** to translate **qahal**—the assembly of Israel before God, especially as "the assembly of the LORD." This created a strong association:

- Ekklesia = the **gathered people of God** in the Old Testament.

- Not just any crowd, but the community summoned by God's covenant.

So by the time of Jesus and the apostles, **ekklesia** already carried Scripture-shaped echoes for Greek-speaking Jews: it could name **Israel gathered** under God's word.

2.2. Ekklesia on Jesus' lips and in Acts

Jesus uses the word ekklesia a few times in the Gospels:

- He speaks of building **"my ekklesia"**—His assembly—on the confession that He is the Messiah.

- He gives instructions for dealing with sin "in the ekklesia," implying a concrete, local gathering that can hear and act.

In Acts and the letters, ekklesia becomes the standard word for:

- Local **congregations** of believers in particular cities.

- The **whole** community of those who belong to Christ across places and times.

The same word can refer to:

- "The ekklesia in Corinth" (a particular local gathering).

- "The ekklesia of God," "the body of Christ," or the ekklesia "throughout Judea, Galilee, and Samaria" (the broader people of God).

In one place, a secular mob in Ephesus is also called an ekklesia, reminding us that the word itself still simply means **assembly**; what makes it "church" is **who is calling and for what**.

3. From "assembly" to "church": what we lost and gained

Our English word **"church"** is a later term, drawn from words meaning "belonging to the Lord." It is not a wrong translation of ekklesia, but it can hide some of the original emphasis.

3.1. Church as building versus ekklesia as people

In common speech:

- "Church" often means a **building** ("I'll meet you at the church").

- It can mean an **institution** or denomination ("the church teaches...").

Ekklesia, by contrast, always refers to **people gathered**. Buildings can burn; institutions can restructure; the ekklesia remains the **assembly of those called by God in Christ**. When the New Testament speaks of "the church," it means:

- People who have been called out of darkness into God's light.

- People who gather around Christ's word and table.

- People who belong to one another as members of a body.

The "church" is not where you go; it is **who you are together**.

3.2. Church as event: gathering, not just label

Because qahal and ekklesia emphasize **gathering**, they highlight that "church" is also an **event**:

- When believers assemble for worship, prayer, teaching, and the Lord's Supper, they are **being** the ekklesia in a particular place and time.

- The New Testament can speak of "coming together as ekklesia," treating the actual gathering as a key expression of their identity.

This does not mean the church ceases to exist between meetings. It means that gathering is not optional extra; it is **central** to what the church is.

4. God's new qahal: continuity and newness

When the New Testament uses ekklesia for the community of Jesus-followers, it is not inventing an entirely new idea. It is picking up the Old

Testament's **qahal of the LORD** and saying:

- God's people are still those whom He **calls and gathers**.

- But now this people is defined by **Jesus the Messiah**, crucified and risen.

- Jews and Gentiles together, by faith, are joined into **one new humanity**, one ekklesia.

There is both **continuity** and **freshness**:

- Continuity: the same God, the same pattern of calling and gathering, the same emphasis on being a people around His presence and word.

- Freshness: the new covenant in Christ's blood, the gift of the Spirit, and the inclusion of the nations in ways hinted at but not fully realized before.

Some New Testament passages even speak of Israel in the wilderness as an ekklesia, reinforcing the link between the old assembly and the new.

5. The ekklesia as Christ's body and God's temple

The New Testament reaches for strong images to describe the ekklesia:

- **Body of Christ** – many members, one body, with Christ as head.

- **Temple of the Holy Spirit** – God's presence dwelling in and among His people.

- **Holy nation, royal priesthood, people for His own possession** – language originally used of Israel, now applied to the church.

These images deepen the basic meaning of ekklesia:

- The church is not just any gathering; it is Christ's **own body in the world**, representing Him.

- The church is not just a religious club; it is God's **dwelling place**, a living temple made of people.

- The church is not a loose network of individuals; it is a **people** with a shared identity and calling.

To speak of the church as ekklesia is to say: **Christ gathers a people to be His visible presence, together.**

6. How our language can flatten "church"

Our ways of speaking can flatten or distort what qahal and ekklesia meant.

- We treat "church" as a **place** rather than a people.

- We imagine "church" as a **service** to attend, rather than a community to which we belong and in which we participate.

- We talk about "going to church" without thinking as much about "being the church" in daily life.

- We accept **solitary Christianity** as normal, even though the New Testament assumes believers are woven into an ekklesia.

Recovering qahal and ekklesia can gently challenge these habits. It reminds us that:

- God's plan is not to save isolated individuals and send them off alone.

- He is forming a **people**, an assembly, a body, a family.

- To belong to Christ is to belong to His people; there is no other version.

7. What did it say first—and how can we hear it now?

If we listen back:

- **Qahal** said: a **summoned assembly**—a people gathered by God's call for worship, covenant, decision, and action.

- **Ekklesia** said: a **called-out gathering**—the community of those whom God has called in Christ, assembled in His name, both locally and across time and space.

For us, hearing these words can:

- Reinforce that "church" is primarily **people**, not place.

- Re-center our idea of church life on **gathering around God's word, table, and presence**, not only on programs or personalities.

- Remind us that Christian faith is **personal but not private**—it is lived as part of a people.

Try it yourself

Here are a few ways to let qahal and ekklesia reshape your sense of "church":

1. **Read a key Old Testament assembly scene**

- For example, read Deuteronomy 5 or Joshua 24.

- Notice what the people do when they assemble (listen, respond, renew covenant).

- Ask: How should this shape what we expect when we gather as church?

1. **Walk through a New Testament letter with "ekklesia" high-lighted**

- Choose 1 Corinthians or Ephesians.

- Mark each occurrence of "church" (ekklesia).

- Note how often the instructions are **community-focused** rather than addressed to isolated individuals.

1. **Reframe how you speak about church for a week**

- Try saying "when we gather as church" instead of "when we go to church."

- Think and pray about your local congregation as an **ekklesia**—a people called and assembled by God.

- Ask: What is one concrete way I can contribute to the life of this gathered people?

As you practice, "church" can slowly recover its original shape: **God's people gathered**—called out, called together, and sent into the world as the living echo of His presence and grace.

Part IV

Sin, Salvation, and the Good News

Books by Rene'

Chapter 17

Missing the Mark

Sin (Chata' / Hamartia)

Most people today hear the word **"sin"** and think of a private moral failure, a religious rule broken, or a guilty feeling. In English, "sin" can sound like a purely **legal** category ("you broke the law") or a purely **internal** one ("I feel bad"). The Bible's main words for sin, however—**chata'** in Hebrew and **hamartia** in Greek—start with a different picture: **missing the mark**, failing to hit the target we were made for. That failure is personal and relational before it is legal; it is about **turning away from God** and twisting the good.

This chapter asks: What did **chata'** and **hamartia** say first? How did Israel and the early church use these words, and how does our flat English "sin" sometimes hide what is at stake?

1. Sin in ancient Israel: chata' as missing the goal

The basic Hebrew verb **chata'** ( )□□□□□□has a concrete root meaning: **to miss**—as when a warrior misses a target. From there, it comes to mean:

- To **fail**, go wrong, miss the way.

- To **do wrong**, to **sin** against God or others.

The related noun forms carry the sense of:

- **Sin** (the act).

- **Sin-offering** (the sacrifice dealing with sin).

- Sometimes even **guilt** or **consequence**.

In Israel's Scriptures, chata' is not simply "breaking a rule." It is:

- **Missing the mark** of God's good design.

- **Failing** in loyalty to the covenant.

- **Wronging** God and neighbor.

You can chata' **against God**, but also **against a person**: sin is always relational.

1.1. Sin as act, state, and stain

The Old Testament uses chata' language in several overlapping ways:

- **Acts**: specific wrong deeds (lying, violence, idolatry).

- **State**: "we have sinned" as a confession of ongoing waywardness.

- **Stain / weight**: sin can be "on" someone, carried or borne, needing removal.

Sacrificial laws talk about bearing or **carrying away** sin. This suggests that sin is not only what we **do**, but something that **clings** and **accumulates**, affecting people and places. It creates a need for **cleansing** as well as for forgiveness.

1.2. Sin against the covenant

Within Israel's covenant, chata' is often linked to **unfaithfulness**:

- Worshiping other gods.

- Trusting in idols or foreign powers instead of YHWH.

- Ignoring justice and mercy.

Sin here is not a random list of infractions; it is **breaking relationship** with the God who rescued and claimed Israel. The law gives shape to the relationship, so breaking the law matters—but at its heart, sin is **covenant betrayal**.

2. Sin in Greek: hamartia as missing the target

The Greek noun **hamartia** (ἁμαρτία) and verb **hamartanō** also carry the basic sense of **missing a mark** or **failing**. In classical usage they can refer to:

- An **error**, mistake, or misjudgment.

- A **failure** to achieve a goal.

- Wrongdoing or **offense**.

In the **Greek Old Testament** (Septuagint), hamartia is used heavily to translate **chata'** and related words. This means that by the time of the New Testament, hamartia carries the **biblical freight** of sin as:

- Missing God's design.

- Violating His commands.

- Falling short of His glory.

3. Hamartia in the New Testament: sin as power and act

New Testament writers use **hamartia** in ways that echo the Old Testament and also develop the theme.

3.1. Sin as a power or realm

In some passages, "sin" is almost personified:

- Sin **reigns** or **rules**.

- People can be **slaves** of sin.

- Sin is a power that **dwells in** human beings.

Here, hamartia is not just a list of wrong acts; it is a **reign** or **domain**. To be "under sin" is to live in a sphere where God's will is resisted and self is at the center.

This lines up with our earlier chapters on **flesh**: sin uses human weakness to dominate. It also echoes the Old Testament sense of sin as something that **clings** and **spreads**, not just isolated mistakes.

3.2. Sin as act and guilt

At the same time, hamartia still names **concrete acts**:

- Specific behaviors that fall short of love for God and neighbor.

- Violations of God's law—whether that law is known in detail (for Israel) or in conscience (for Gentiles).

New Testament writers can speak of:

- **Committing** sins (plural).

- Being **forgiven** sins.

- Having sins **washed away**.

So hamartia is both:

- A **power** that enslaves, and

- A set of **acts** that express that power and incur guilt.

4. Sin and the law: more than rule-breaking

Because "sin" and "law" are closely connected in Paul, it is easy to reduce sin to rule-breaking. Scripture's picture is more nuanced.

- The **law** reveals what is right and wrong.

- It can even **increase** sin by making rebellion more pointed.

- But sin is fundamentally about **falling short of the glory of God**—failing to reflect His character as His image-bearers.

Sin includes:

- Wrong acts (transgressing commands).

- **Twisted desires** (disordered loves).

- **Warped thinking** (believing lies).

- A **bent will** (resisting God's good).

The commandments help us see sin, but sin is deeper than "I broke a rule." It is more like **aiming at the wrong target, or refusing to aim at all.**

5. Time and audience: what "sin" sounded like then

For ancient Israelites:

- "Sin" language sounded like **unfaithfulness to the God who brought us out of Egypt.**

- It evoked images of **missing the way, straying, breaking covenant**, and accumulating **uncleanness** that required sacrifice and repentance.

For Jews and Gentiles in the first-century Mediterranean world:

- Hamartia carried both the **moral** sense (wrongdoing) and the **religious** sense (offense against God).

- In Christian preaching, it came to name the **universal human condition**—Jew and Gentile alike under sin's power and in need of God's rescue.

Today, many people hear "sin" as:

- A churchy word for things that break **arbitrary rules**, or

- A label for **private moral slips** in a narrow list (especially sexual matters).

The biblical picture is wider and deeper: sin is a **fundamental misdirection of the human person and community** away from God and His good purposes.

6. Flattening: when "sin" becomes too small

Our English word "sin" can flatten chata' and hamartia in at least three ways.

6.1. Sin as only legal guilt

If we treat sin solely as **breaking laws**, we may:

- Focus on fear of penalty rather than on **broken relationship**.

- Miss the way sin **damages us**, others, and creation.

- Think that avoiding certain obvious "sins" means we are basically fine.

Biblically, sin always has a **relational dimension**: it is against God, against His image in others, and against our own calling.

6.2. Sin as only private moral failure

If we see sin only as:

- Personal moral missteps,

- Private, interior issues,

we can overlook:

- **Structural** and **communal** sins (injustice, oppression, idols of a culture).

- The way sin operates as a **power** beyond individual choices.

- Our need not just for forgiveness, but for being **freed** from sin's reign.

Scripture talks about sinful **hearts**, **habits**, and **systems**, not only isolated acts.

6.3. Sin as only "naughty" behavior

In some church cultures, "sin" is used mostly for a short list of behaviors and becomes almost a joke word ("sinful desserts"). That can dull our sense that:

- Sin is deadly serious—it leads to **death**.

- Sin is the **reason** for the cross.

- Sin is what Christ came to **deal with decisively**, not to manage politely.

When "sin" sounds trivial, the **good news** of salvation from sin also shrinks.

7. What did it say first—and how can we hear it now?

If we go back to the roots:

- **Chata'** first meant **missing the mark**, failing to hit the target. It came to mean **acting and living off-target** with respect to God's covenant and design.

- **Hamartia** picked up that sense of **failure and offense**, and in the New Testament names both:

- our **acts** of missing God's way, and

- the **power** of sin that enslaves and distorts.

For us, that means:

- When we see "sin," we can think **"off-target life"**—failing to love God and neighbor; failing to image God's character.

- When we confess sin, we can bring not only specific wrong acts but also the **bent desires and patterns** that lie beneath them.

- When we hear that Christ saves us from sin, we can understand that as both **forgiveness of guilt** and **liberation from sin's rule**, not just a clean legal record.

This sets us up for the chapters that follow:

- To see "iniquity" and "lawlessness" as deeper ways of talking about sin's twisting and rebellion.

- To see "peace" and "salvation" not merely as inner calm and ticket to heaven, but as **wholeness and rescue** from this misdirected life into the life we were made for.

Try it yourself

Here are a few simple ways to let chata' and hamartia reshape your understanding of sin:

1. **Rewrite a familiar verse with "missing the mark" in mind**

- Take a verse like "all have sinned and fall short of the glory of God."

- Paraphrase: "all have **missed the target** of reflecting God's glory."

- Ask: How does that change how I see what's wrong with the world—and with me?

1. **Trace sin as power and acts in one chapter**

- Read Romans 6 or another sin-focused chapter.

- Mark where "sin" sounds like a **power** and where it sounds like **acts**.

- Notice how both are in view: what we do and what we are under.

1. **Name a "missed mark" in your own life**

- Instead of only listing broken rules, ask:

- Where have I **aimed my life** at the wrong target (success, approval, comfort)?

- Where has that led me to **miss** love of God and neighbor?

- Let your confession move from "I broke a rule" to "I have been off-target—turn me back."

As you practice, "sin" will begin to sound less like a thin religious label and more like what the Bible always meant: a **tragic misdirection** of human life that Christ has come to forgive, heal, and finally set right.

Chapter 18

Iniquity and Lawlessness

Avon, Pesha', and Anomia

Chapter 17 traced "sin" as **missing the mark**—falling short of the life we were made for. Scripture, however, uses other words that zoom in on **how** sin works and **what it becomes** when it sets hard: **avon**, **pesha'**, and, in the New Testament, **anomia**. These terms speak of **twisting**, **rebellion**, and **lawlessness**. They help us see that sin is not only failure; it is also **defiance** and **distortion**.

This chapter asks: What did **avon, pesha'**, and **anomia** say first? How do they deepen the picture of sin beyond "missing the mark," and how does our flat English ("iniquity," "transgression," "lawlessness") sometimes hide their force?

1. Three Hebrew words: chata', pesha', avon

Hebrew uses several major words for sin. Together they paint a progression:

- **Chata'** – missing the mark, failing to hit the target.

- **Pesha'** – **transgression** or **rebellion**, crossing a boundary on purpose.

- **Avon** – **iniquity**, the **twisted, warped condition** that sin produces.

We looked at chata' already. Here we focus on **pesha'** and **avon**.

1.1. Pesha': rebellious transgression

The noun **pesha'** ( )□□□□□□□□often appears in contexts of:

- **Rebellion** against a king or overlord.

- **Breach of covenant**—breaking terms of a solemn relationship.

- **Violation of trust**, like betraying a neighbor.

Pesha' is not an accidental slip. It is **willful disobedience**, a conscious stepping over a known line. To **transgress** in this sense is more like treason than a minor infraction. It is to **throw off rightful authority**.

This word highlights the **relational betrayal** in sin: not just "I broke a rule," but "I broke faith with someone to whom I owed loyalty."

1.2. Avon: iniquity as twistedness and burden

The Hebrew **avon** ( )□□□□□□is usually translated **"iniquity."** Word studies describe it as:

- **Warped, bent, or twisted** behavior and character.

- The **crookedness** that results from repeated sin.

- A combination of **guilt**, **corruption**, and often the **consequences** that follow.

Avon can refer to:

- The **iniquitous act itself**.

- The **state** of being twisted and guilty.

- The **burden** or **punishment** that rests on someone because of that iniquity.

This is why some key passages can speak of:

- Bearing one's **iniquity**.

- God **visiting** iniquity.

- God **forgiving** iniquity and choosing not to remember it.

Avon tells us that sin does not just break a rule; it **bends** the sinner. Over time, repeated rebellion warps character and relationships, leaving a kind of **weight** that must be dealt with.

2. Iniquity, transgression, and forgiveness

Important confessional texts in the Old Testament pile these words together:

"[The LORD] forgives **iniquity, transgression**, and **sin...**"

Here:

- **Sin (chata')** – missing the mark.

- **Transgression (pesha')** – deliberate rebellion.

- **Iniquity (avon)** – the twisted state and burden that result.

This triple formula is not mere repetition. It says:

- God forgives **failures**.

- God forgives **defiance**.

- God can deal with the **distortion and weight** that sin creates.

At the same time, these words remind us that sin has **layers**: acts, attitudes, and deepened patterns.

3. From avon and pesha' to anomia: lawlessness in the New Testament

The New Testament uses several Greek words to express these ideas. For "transgression" and "iniquity," one key term is **anomia** (ἀνομία), often translated **"lawlessness"** or sometimes "iniquity."

- **Nomos** is "law."

- **A-nomia** is literally **"without law"** or "against law."

Lexicons describe anomia as:

- **Violation of law**, disregard for God's will.

- A **state** of being lawless, not just isolated acts.

- A principle of **living as if God has no authority**.

Just as hamartia can be both act and power, so anomia can:

- Describe **individual lawless deeds**.

- Name a **pattern** or **realm** of lawlessness—a way of life that rejects God's rule.

Some New Testament passages even define sin as **lawlessness** ("sin is anomia"), stressing that persistent sin is a settled attitude of **refusing God's revealed will**.

4. Lawlessness as rebellion made normal

When the New Testament speaks of anomia, it often has in view:

- People who **practice** lawlessness, not just stumble.

- A "mystery of lawlessness" already at work—a hidden process by which rejection of God's authority grows and spreads.

- A sharp contrast between **righteousness** and **lawlessness**, making it impossible for light and darkness to have real fellowship.

In some apocalyptic passages, there appears:

- A **"man of lawlessness"**—a figure in whom rebellion reaches a kind of climax.

- A description of times when **lawlessness increases** and love grows cold.

Here we see pesha' (rebellion) and avon (twistedness) in Greek dress:

- **Pesha'** – the act of defying God's law and covenant.

- **Avon** – the twisted state that grows from repeated defiance.

- **Anomia** – a way of life and a social atmosphere where God's law is ignored or despised.

5. Iniquity and lawlessness today: how we flatten or dodge them

Our English words "iniquity," "transgression," and "lawlessness" can sound archaic or abstract.

- "Iniquity" may sound like a fancy synonym for "sin," without the idea of **twisting and corruption**.

- "Transgression" may sound like a minor parking violation, not **covenant treason**.

- "Lawlessness" may sound like "breaking the rules," not a **principle of rejecting God's rule**.

When we flatten these words:

- We may underestimate how **personal and defiant** sin can be.

- We may overlook how repeated sin **reshapes** us and our communities.

- We may think of "lawlessness" only in others (criminals, corrupt societies), not in our own tendency to **do what is right in our own eyes**.

The biblical vocabulary is trying to wake us up:

- You are not only capable of missing the mark; you are capable of **rebellion**.

- That rebellion, unchecked, will **warp** you and those around you.

- Entire cultures can slide into **anomia**, where God's ways are no longer acknowledged as binding.

6. What did it say first—and how can we hear it now?

If we listen to these words as they were first used:

- **Pesha'** says: **rebellion**, willful transgression, betrayal of trust.

- **Avon** says: **iniquity**, the twisted, burdened condition and guilt that flow from repeated sin.

- **Anomia** says: **lawlessness**, a state and practice of living without regard for God's will.

Together with chata' and hamartia, they deepen the diagnosis:

- We **miss the mark** (chata', hamartia).

- We can **rebel on purpose** (pesha').

- That rebellion can **warp us** (avon).

- And, unchecked, it can harden into a **way of life**—anomia—that resists God's rule.

For us, that means:

- Confession can move beyond "I made a mistake" to "I have **resisted You**," and "I see how that resistance has **twisted** me."

- We can recognize lawlessness not only in extreme evil "out there" but wherever we or our communities choose **self-rule over God's rule**.

- We can hear the gospel as good news not only of **forgiveness for acts**, but of **cleansing from iniquity** and **redemption from lawlessness**—a deep re-straightening of bent lives.

7. Try it yourself

Here are some ways to let these words sink in:

1. **Read a triple-word confession**

- Find a verse or prayer that mentions "sin, transgression, and iniquity" together.

- Paraphrase it as "missing the mark, rebelling, and becoming twisted."

- Notice how comprehensive the confession becomes.

1. **Name one area of "twisting"**

- Ask: Where has repeated compromise or disobedience **bent** me—my reactions, desires, or habits?

- Bring that not just as a list of acts but as **avon**—a pattern needing cleansing and unbending.

1. **Watch for lawlessness in yourself and your setting**

- When you encounter a passage about "lawlessness," ask:

- How does this show up in **me** (living as if God does not get to say)?

- How does it show up in my **community** (what we normalize or excuse)?

- Let that awareness drive you, not to despair, but to the One who "redeems us from all lawlessness and purifies for himself a people eager to do good."

As these words regain their depth, "sin" will no longer sound generic. You will hear, instead, a layered diagnosis—and be ready to appreciate, more fully, the layered richness of the words that come next: **shalom** and **salvation**.

Chapter 19

Peace as Wholeness

Shalom and Eirēnē

When many of us hear **"peace,"** we think of a cease-fire: no fighting, no noise, no trouble for a moment. The Bible's key words for peace—**shalom** in Hebrew and **eirēnē** in Greek—are far bigger. They name **wholeness**, **right relationship**, and **everything in its proper place** under God's blessing. They describe not just the **absence of conflict**, but the **presence of full, ordered life.**

This chapter asks: What did **shalom** and **eirēnē** say first? How do they move beyond "no conflict" to "nothing missing, nothing broken," and how does that deepen what we mean by "peace with God"?

1. Shalom in the Old Testament: completeness, not just calm

The Hebrew word **shalom** ( )□□□□□□□comes from a root meaning **wholeness** or **completeness**. Word studies describe shalom as:

- **Completeness, soundness, welfare, peace.**

- A state where nothing essential is **missing** and nothing is **out of joint.**

- Harmony in multiple dimensions: with God, with others, within oneself, and with creation.

Shalom can refer to:

- **Personal well-being** – health, safety, security.

- **Relational harmony** – peace between individuals or nations.

- **Material sufficiency** – prosperity or "all is well" with one's affairs.

- **Covenant blessing** – life as God intends it for His people.

So when someone greets another with "shalom," they are not just saying "no war today." They are wishing—and, in biblical blessings, invoking—**fullness of life under God's favor**.

2. Shalom and God's covenant: peace as gift and goal

In Israel's Scriptures, shalom is tightly linked to **covenant**:

- God promises shalom as part of His **blessing** when His people walk in His ways.

- Prophets announce coming shalom when God restores His scattered people.

- One title for God is "the LORD is peace," and a key priestly blessing ends with "give you peace."

At the same time, shalom is **fragile** in a rebellious world:

- False prophets cry "Peace, peace" when there is no peace, denying the seriousness of injustice and idolatry.

- True shalom requires **right relationship**, not just quiet circumstances.

This means biblical peace is never **cheap**. It is not attained by ignoring wrongdoing or pretending everything is fine. It comes when God **sets things right**—forgiving, healing, judging, and restoring.

3. Eirēnē in the New Testament: joining what was divided

The Greek word **eirēnē** (εἰρήνη) is often used in everyday Greek for:

- The **opposite of war**—a state of national tranquility.

- **Harmony** between individuals.

- Conditions where **prosperity and rest** can flourish because conflict has ceased.

In the Greek Old Testament, eirēnē is used to translate **shalom**, carrying over its deeper sense of **wholeness and well-being**. Lexicons note that eirēnē is related to a verb meaning "to **join** or **bind together** what was separated," so peace is:

- Things **put back together**.

- A state of **reconciliation** and **integration**, not just a pause in hostilities.

In the New Testament, eirēnē inherits the full biblical range:

- **Peace with God** – reconciliation through Christ.

- **Peace within** – a settled heart anchored in God's care.

- **Peace with others** – unity in the body of Christ and love across divides.

- **Peace as the mark of God's kingdom** – "righteousness, peace, and joy in the Holy Spirit."

4. Jesus the bringer and embodiment of peace

The New Testament applies shalom/eirēne language directly to Jesus:

- At His birth, the angels announce "peace on earth" to those on whom God's favor rests.

- He is called the **Prince of Peace**, fulfilling prophetic hopes.

- He says to His disciples, "My peace I give to you," distinguishing His peace from what the world offers.

- A key letter says, simply, "He **himself** is our peace."

This peace is:

- **Objective** – Christ's death removes hostility between God and humans, creating genuine **reconciliation**.

- **Relational** – Christ brings Jew and Gentile into one body, breaking down dividing walls.

- **Experiential** – believers can know a "peace of God" that guards hearts and minds even in trouble.

So peace is not just something Christ **gives**; in a real sense, it is what He **is** and **does** as He restores right relationship between God and people and among people themselves.

5. Peace now and not yet

Biblical peace has a **"now and not yet"** character:

- **Now** – Those who trust Christ are said to have **peace with God**, an end to enmity. They are called to live at peace with others as far as it depends on them and to let the peace of Christ rule in their hearts.

- **Not yet** – Full shalom awaits the renewal of all things: a world where justice and righteousness dwell, where swords become plowshares, and where God wipes away every tear.

This keeps us from two mistakes:

- **Over-spiritualizing** peace, as if it were only an inner feeling, unrelated to justice and reconciliation in the world.

- **Over-politicizing** peace, as if it were only cease-fires and treaties, without attention to reconciliation with God and inner transformation.

Biblical shalom/eirēnē is **whole-person, whole-world** peace.

6. How our language flattens "peace"

Our word "peace" can be too small.

- It often means just **absence of conflict**: no fighting in the house, no war in the headlines.

- It may mean a **feeling** of calm, even if life is unjust or misaligned.

- It can be used to bless escapism: "I just want some peace," meaning "I want to avoid people and problems."

Compared to shalom/eirēnē, this is thin. Biblical peace:

- Requires **truth and justice**, not denial.

- Includes **right relationship** with God and neighbor.

- Has a **positive shape**: wholeness, harmony, flourishing.

If we reduce peace to "no one is yelling," we may mistake **quiet injustice** for shalom.

7. What did it say first—and how can we hear it now?

If we listen back:

- **Shalom** said: **wholeness, completeness, well-being, right relationships, and harmony** under God's blessing—personally, socially, and even cosmically.

- **Eirēnē** said: **joining together what was divided**, reconciliation and rest that reflect and extend shalom.

For us, that means:

- When we read "peace," we can think: **"everything put right and held together under God"**, not only "no conflict."

- When we hear "peace with God," we can remember that this is **real reconciliation**—the end of enmity and the beginning of restored relationship.

- When we pray for peace, we can ask not only for quiet, but for **truth, justice, healing, and restored relationships.**

And when Jesus says, "Blessed are the **peacemakers**," we can hear:

- Not just "those who avoid fights," but

- Those who actively **join what is broken**, heal divisions, and seek shalom in line with God's kingdom.

8. Try it yourself

Here are a few ways to let shalom and eirēnē reshape your sense of peace:

1. **Rewrite "peace" passages with "wholeness" in mind**

- Take a familiar verse about peace (for example, "The peace of God… will guard your hearts and minds").

- Paraphrase "peace" as "the wholeness and steadiness God gives."

- Ask: What situations in my life need that kind of wholeness?

1. **Pray the priestly blessing for someone**

- Use the words, "The LORD lift up His face upon you and give you peace."

- As you say "peace," consciously mean "fullness of life in right relationship with God and others."

- Let that deepen how you bless them.

1. **Practice one concrete act of peacemaking**

- Identify a relationship or context where there is tension or fracture.

- Ask: What small step could I take toward **repair**, not just toward silence?

- See that step as participating in Christ's work of **shalom**.

As you do, "peace" will start to sound less like a fragile truce and more like what the Bible meant from the beginning: **the deep, sturdy wholeness that comes when God puts things right and holds them together in love.**

Chapter 20

Rescue and Healing

Salvation (Yasha' / Sōzō)

Ask a random person what "salvation" means, and you may hear: "going to heaven when you die" or "forgiveness so you don't go to hell." The Bible's words for salvation do include rescue from judgment and hope beyond death. But they start earlier and broader. The main Hebrew root **yasha'** and the Greek verb **sōzō** speak of **rescue, safety, healing, and making whole** in many dimensions of life—physical, social, and spiritual.

This chapter asks: What did **yasha'** and **sōzō** say first? How does that widen our picture of salvation from a narrow "afterlife" ticket to a rich **rescue-and-restoration** project God is working in the world?

1. Yasha' and yeshuah in the Old Testament: making wide, making safe

The Hebrew verb **yasha'** ( )□□□□□□literally carries the idea of being **wide, open, free**—as opposed to being hemmed in, trapped, or under threat. From there it comes to mean:

- To **save, deliver, rescue, bring to safety**.

- To **liberate** from danger, oppression, or defeat.

- To **give victory**.

Lexicons list uses like:

- Being **rescued** from enemies in battle.

- Being **delivered** from distress or trouble.

- Being **saved** from moral or spiritual danger.

The related noun **yeshuah** ( )□□□□□□□□□□means:

- **Salvation, deliverance, rescue, help, victory.**

When Moses tells Israel to "stand firm and see the salvation of the LORD," the word is **yeshuah**: the concrete, dramatic rescue God is about to work at the sea.

So in the Old Testament, salvation language is very **earthy**:

- God saves from **armies, famine, illness, exile**.

- Those rescues also point to a deeper pattern: God is the one who brings His people into **freedom and life**, not bondage and ruin.

Salvation is not just about where someone goes after death; it is about **how God acts now** to bring people out of tight places into spacious ones.

2. Sōzō and sōtēria in the New Testament: save, heal, make whole

The Greek verb **sōzō** (σῴζω) and noun **sōtēria** (σωτηρία) pick up and expand this rescue theme.

Lexicons summarize sōzō as:

- To **save, rescue, deliver** from danger.

- To **heal, make well, restore to health**.

- To **preserve, keep safe**.

In the New Testament, sōzō is used for:

- **Physical rescue** – from storms, danger, or death.

- **Healing** – a woman "is saved" from her disease, meaning healed; someone's faith "has saved" them, in the sense of healing.

- **Deliverance** from demonic oppression.

- **Spiritual salvation** – rescue from sin, judgment, and lostness into life with God.

The noun **sōtēria** similarly means:

- **Deliverance, preservation, safety, salvation**, including what we call "Messianic salvation": the blessings Christ brings now and in the age to come.

So when the New Testament says "save" and "salvation," it draws on a word that naturally covers:

- Being pulled from the water.

- Being healed from disease.

- Being freed from unclean spirits.

- Being brought from the path of death and judgment onto the path of true life.

3. Salvation from what? Danger, enemies, sin, and death

Across both Testaments, salvation answers to particular **dangers**.

- In many Old Testament stories, God saves from **external enemies**—Egyptian oppressors, attacking armies, hostile nations.

- He also saves from **disasters** and **distresses** (famine, plague, exile).

- As the story unfolds, salvation is increasingly tied to rescue from **sin** and its consequences: guilt, shame, hard hearts, and the threat of God's judgment.

The New Testament gathers these threads and focuses them on Christ:

- He saves people from their **sins**—guilt, power, and eventual penalty.

- He saves from **God's wrath**—the righteous judgment against evil.

- He saves from **death**—first in foretaste (resurrections and signs), finally in His own resurrection and promised future resurrection for His people.

- He saves from **lostness**—life lived far from God's purpose, heading toward destruction.

So biblical salvation is:

- **From**: enemies, bondage, sin, judgment, death, meaninglessness.

- **For**: freedom, holiness, peace, life with God, new creation.

4. Salvation as present, ongoing, and future

The Bible speaks of salvation in **three tenses**:

- **You have been saved** – a completed act (justification, new birth, being brought into reconciled relationship with God).

- **You are being saved** – an ongoing process (sanctification, being freed from sin's power and healed of its effects).

- **You will be saved** – a future hope (final rescue at judgment, resurrection, full participation in the renewed creation).

This reflects the breadth of yasha'/sōzō:

- God **has** delivered us from our greatest enemies in Christ's cross and resurrection.

- God **is** delivering us as the Spirit works in us.

- God **will** deliver us fully when Christ returns.

If we talk about salvation only in the past ("I got saved") or only in the future ("I hope I go to heaven"), we miss that salvation is also a **present journey** of being made whole.

5. Salvation and healing: being made whole, not just acquitted

Because sōzō is often used for **healing**, it reminds us:

- Salvation is not just a **legal acquittal** (though it includes being declared righteous).

- It is also a **healing and restoration** of the person and community.

Think of:

- Broken bodies made whole.

- Broken relationships reconciled.

- Twisted hearts straightened.

- Shattered communities rebuilt.

In terms from earlier chapters:

- Salvation touches **soul (nephesh/psychē)**—life and identity.

- **Spirit (ruach/pneuma)**—our inner life and connection with God.

- **Flesh and body (basar, sarx, sōma)**—our embodied existence.

- **Heart (lev/kardia)**—thoughts, desires, will.

- **Humanity and image**—our calling to reflect God.

Salvation is God's work to **restore His image-bearers** and their world.

6. How our language can flatten "salvation"

Our English "salvation" can easily be flattened in two ways.

6.1. Only afterlife, not this life

If salvation means only:

- "what happens after I die,"

we may:

- Neglect the **present work** God wants to do in us and through us.

- Treat this life as just **waiting room** for heaven.

- Think of the gospel as mainly an **insurance policy**, not as good news for today's fears, sins, and hurts.

Biblical salvation begins **now**: new birth, new heart, new Spirit, new community.

6.2. Only private, not communal and cosmic

If salvation is only about:

- "my personal forgiveness,"

we can miss:

- God's purpose to save a **people**, not just isolated individuals.

- His plan to renew **creation** itself—freeing it from decay and futility.

- The way salvation should **spill over** into how we treat neighbors, enemies, and the earth.

Scripture ends, not with souls escaping, but with **heaven and earth united**, a healed creation in which God lives with His people. Salvation is big enough for the whole world.

7. What did it say first—and how can we hear it now?

If we listen at the roots:

- **Yasha'** said: to **make wide, free, safe**—to rescue, deliver, save, give victory.

- **Yeshuah** said: **salvation, deliverance, rescue, help**—God's concrete acts of saving His people.

- **Sōzō / sōtēria** said: to **save, rescue, heal, preserve**, and the **state** of rescue and well-being that results.

For us, that means:

- When we see "save," we can think: **"rescue and make whole"**—from danger, sin, and death into life with God.

- When we see "salvation," we can hear: **"God's full rescue project"**—past, present, and future.

- When we speak of being "saved," we can remember: it is not only about a future destination, but about being **brought into God's**

life and mission now.

This ties the whole book together:

- The God who named Himself to Moses, who gathered a people, who came among us in Jesus, now works by His Spirit to **save**—to rescue, cleanse, heal, and restore His image-bearers and His world.

8. Try it yourself

Here are a few ways to let yasha' and sōzō reshape your sense of salvation:

1. **Ask "saved from what, for what?" in familiar verses**

- Take a verse about salvation (for example, "by grace you have been saved").

- Ask: From what dangers or lostness? For what kind of life and purpose?

- Write a one-sentence paraphrase that answers both.

1. **Notice where "save" means "heal" in the Gospels**

- Read a healing story and look for the word "made well" or "healed"—often it's sōzō.

- Reflect on how physical healing illustrates what God wants to do in your **whole life**.

1. **Pray a broad salvation prayer**

- Instead of only asking God to forgive sins, also ask Him to:

- Rescue from specific patterns of bondage.

- Heal particular wounds.

- Restore broken relationships.

- Use you as an agent of His rescue in someone else's life.

As you do, "salvation" will become less like a thin ticket and more like what it has always been in Scripture: **God's wide, deep rescue—pulling people out of tight, deadly places into the spacious, whole life of His kingdom.**

Grace, Faith, and Faithfulness (Ḥen / Charis, 'Aman / Pistis)

If you ask what holds the whole Christian message together, many would answer: **grace** and **faith**. But in English those words can sound thin. "Grace" may mean elegance, a polite prayer before meals, or vague leniency. "Faith" may mean positive feelings, blind leap, or "believing hard." The Bible's main words—ḥen and **charis** for grace, 'aman and **pistis** for faith/faithfulness—are sturdier. They point to **generous favor** and **steady trust/loyalty** lived out over time.

This chapter asks: What did **ḥen / charis** and 'aman / **pistis** say first? How do they weave together into the pattern "by grace through faith," and how does our flat English sometimes pull them apart?

1. Grace in the Old Testament: ḥen as favor and kindness

The Hebrew noun ḥen ( )□□□and related verb forms describe:

- **Favor** – being pleased with someone, looking kindly on them.

- **Kindness** shown to someone who is not entitled to it.

- The **attractiveness** or charm that awakens goodwill.

When someone "finds ḥen in the eyes" of another, it means:

- They receive **kind regard**.

- They are treated with **kindness or generosity**, often beyond what they deserve or can repay.

When God shows ḥen:

- He looks with **favor** on individuals or the nation.

- He acts with **compassion and generosity**—rescuing, forgiving, providing.

- His favor is often linked to His **steadfast love** and **covenant mercy**, not to human merit.

So ḥen is not a technical theological word; it's everyday language for **favor freely shown**, which becomes a key way of talking about God's kindness.

2. Grace in the New Testament: charis as gift and power

The Greek word **charis** (χάρις) covers:

- **Grace, favor, kindness**.

- A **gift** freely given.

- Sometimes the **thanks** or gratitude that responds to a gift.

In the New Testament, charis becomes the central word for:

- God's **unearned favor** toward sinners in Christ.

- The **gift-character** of salvation: it is by grace, not by works.

- The **ongoing power** God gives to enable obedience and service.

Charis includes:

- **Attitude** – God's gracious disposition toward us.

- **Action** – what He does to save and sustain us.

- **Effect** – the changed lives and gifts that flow from His generosity.

So when the New Testament says we are saved "by grace," it is saying:

- Our rescue is **God's free gift**, rooted in His kindness, not our worthiness.

- The entire movement—from forgiveness to new life—is **charis**, undeserved generosity.

3. Faith and faithfulness in the Old Testament: 'aman

The Hebrew root **'aman** ( )□□□□□ gives us:

- The idea of being **firm, reliable, steady**.

- The word "**amen**" – "it is firm, truly, so be it."

- Concepts of **trust, reliability**, and **faithfulness**.

The related noun forms can mean:

- **Faithfulness** – steadiness over time.

- **Trust** – relying on someone's reliability.

When Scripture calls people to trust God, it is calling them to:

- **Lean their weight** on His reliability.

- Be **firm and steadfast** in allegiance to Him.

- Live in **faithful response** to His faithful character.

Faith, in this sense, is not a fleeting feeling but **steady reliance** and **loyalty** to a trustworthy God.

4. Faith in the New Testament: pistis as trust and loyalty

The Greek noun **pistis** (πίστις) and verb **pisteuō** (πιστεύω) are usually translated **"faith"** and **"believe."** Lexicons summarize pistis as:

- **Trust, confidence, reliance**.

- **Faithfulness, fidelity, loyalty**.

- Sometimes, the "faith" as a **body of teaching** believed.

In the New Testament:

- To "have pistis in" Christ is to **trust Him, entrust oneself** to Him.

- Pistis also names the **ongoing loyalty** that flows from that trust—staying faithful to Christ.

This dual sense means:

- Faith is both **receiving** (empty hands open to God's gift) and **remaining** (staying loyal, continuing in trust).

- When Scripture contrasts faith with works as the basis of justification, it is not playing down obedience; it is insisting that we are made right with God **by trusting His grace in Christ**, not by earning His favor.

Some discussions underline that pistis in many contexts could be rendered **"faithful allegiance"**—a lived, loyal trust in Jesus as Lord.

5. By grace through faith: how the words fit

When the New Testament says we are saved **by grace through faith**:

- **By grace (charis)** – the **source** is God's free, generous favor and action.

- **Through faith (pistis)** – the **means** by which we receive it is trusting, relying, and pledging ourselves to that grace.

This guards two truths:

- We do **not earn** salvation; it is God's gift from start to finish.

- We are not **passive** objects; we are called to **respond** with real trust and ongoing faithfulness.

Grace and faith belong together:

- Grace without faith becomes a **general niceness**—God is kind, but nothing changes.

- Faith without grace becomes **striving**—trying to earn what only God can give.

- Together, they describe a relationship where a generous God gives Himself, and humans respond by entrusting themselves to Him.

6. Flattening: when "grace" and "faith" shrink

Our English usage can flatten these words.

6.1. Grace as vague leniency

If "grace" means only:

- "God being chill about sin,"

we may:

- Treat sin lightly.

- See grace as a **cover** so we can stay the same.

- Miss that grace is also God's **power to transform** and teach us to say no to ungodliness.

Biblical grace **forgives** and **trains**, pardons and reshapes.

6.2. Faith as feelings or mere opinion

If "faith" means:

- A warm feeling about God, or

- Holding certain ideas to be true,

we may:

- Talk about "losing faith" when our feelings change.

- Disconnect "faith" from **trusting obedience**.

Biblical pistis is closer to **loyal trust**—a settled reliance and allegiance that show in life.

7. What did it say first—and how can we hear it now?

Listening back:

- **Ḥen / charis** say: **freely given favor and kindness**—God's generous, unearned gift and help.

- **'Aman / pistis** say: **trust and faithfulness**—steadfast reliance on, and loyalty to, a trustworthy God and His Messiah.

For us, that means:

- When we say we are saved **by grace**, we can remember: everything begins and continues with **God's generous initiative**, not our performance.

- When we speak of **faith**, we can mean: **embracing that grace with trust and letting it shape a loyal life**, not just agreeing with ideas.

- When we hold them together, we can live in the paradox: **we contribute nothing to our rescue, yet we are fully called to respond.**

If earlier chapters have helped you hear words like "Lord," "soul," "church," "sin," and "salvation" more clearly, this chapter invites you to let **grace and faith** recover their weight as well—so that "by grace through faith" becomes not a slogan, but a living description of how a generous God and trusting people meet.

Chapter 22

Righteousness and Justice

Tsedaqah and Dikaiosynē

In many English Bibles, two clusters of words—**"righteousness"** and **"justice"**—sound like different things. "Righteousness" can sound private and religious, about personal morality or inner purity. "Justice" can sound public and social, about courts and politics. In Scripture, the main Hebrew and Greek words—**tsedaqah** and **dikaiosynē**—hold these together. They name a **relational rightness**: being set right with God and living rightly toward others.

This chapter asks: What did **tsedaqah** and **dikaiosynē** say first? How do they unite righteousness and justice, and how does splitting them in English blur what the Bible is calling us to?

1. Tsedaqah in the Old Testament: rightness, generosity, and relationship

The Hebrew word **tsedaqah** (,)□□□□□□□from the root *ts-d-q*, is usually translated **"righteousness."** Word studies describe it as:

- **Right order, rightness, straightness**.

- **Righteousness** in character and behavior.

- **Justice** expressed in concrete actions, often toward the vulnerable.

Tsedaqah shows up in several ways:

- **God's righteousness** – His moral integrity, faithfulness to His promises, and commitment to set things right.

- **Human righteousness** – living in line with God's character and covenant.

- **Practical righteousness** – acts of **generosity and fairness**, especially to the poor, stranger, widow, and orphan.

In many Hebrew and later Jewish contexts, tsedaqah can even mean **charitable giving**—not as an optional extra, but as an expression of **justice**. To be "righteous" is not only to avoid doing wrong; it is to **do right by others**, especially those in need.

Tsedaqah often appears paired with **mishpat** ("justice"):

- God loves **justice and righteousness**.

- Kings and leaders are called to execute **justice and righteousness**.

Together, mishpat and tsedaqah describe a society where:

- Wrong is addressed and put right.

- Relationships and structures are ordered according to God's standards.

- The vulnerable are protected and cared for.

2. Dikaiosynē in the New Testament: righteousness as justice set right

The Greek word **dikaiosynē** (δικαιοσύνη) carries the same family of meanings:

- **Righteousness** – being in the right, according to God's standard.

- **Justice** – what is right and fair in relationships and community.

- **Justification** – being **declared in the right** by God.

In Greek usage, the *dikaios-* family often refers to:

- A **just measure** or standard.

- Acting rightly toward others.

- Legal justice—decisions in court.

In the Greek Old Testament, **dikaiosynē** frequently translates **tsedaqah**, so by the time of the New Testament it naturally means:

- **Right relationship** with God and with others.

- God's own **righteous character and saving justice**.

- The **state** of being set right by God and living in line with that.

When Paul and other writers speak of "the righteousness of God," they can mean:

- God's **upright character and faithfulness**.

- God's **saving action** that sets people right.

- The **gifted status** of those whom God declares righteous in Christ.

"Righteousness" and "justice" are not two different words here; they are two English attempts to capture one deep reality: **right-ordered relationships and actions in line with God's good standard.**

3. God's righteousness: character, promise, and setting things right

In both Testaments, **God** is the ultimate standard of tsedaqah/dikaiosynē.

God's righteousness includes:

- **Moral perfection** – He does what is right, without partiality or corruption.

- **Faithfulness** – He keeps His covenant promises; He can be relied on.

- **Saving justice** – He acts to **put things right** for His people and, ultimately, for the world.

This means "the righteousness of God" is not only a threat ("He will judge") but also:

- A **hope**: He will not let injustice and evil stand forever.

- A **comfort**: He will vindicate the oppressed and marginalized.

- A **gift**: He provides a way for sinners to be set right with Him.

When the New Testament announces that in the gospel "the righteousness of God is revealed," it is saying: God has acted, in Jesus, to **faithfully keep His promises** and **set humans right** with Himself in a way that is just and merciful at once.

4. Our righteousness: gift and calling

The Bible speaks of human righteousness in two key senses.

4.1. Righteousness as gift: being declared right

In key passages, believers are said to be:

- **Justified** – declared righteous, put in the right with God.

- Given **righteousness** apart from works of the law.

- Counted righteous through union with Christ.

Here, righteousness is:

- A **gifted status** before God, not something we earn.

- Based on **Christ's faithfulness and sacrifice**, not our performance.

- Received **by faith**, as we trust God's promise and entrust ourselves to Christ.

This guards the truth that:

- We cannot **climb** to God by our own righteousness.

- We stand accepted because God **sets us right** in Christ.

4.2. Righteousness as practice: living rightly

At the same time, Scripture calls believers to **pursue** righteousness:

- To **hunger and thirst** for righteousness.

- To **practice** righteousness in daily life.

- To live in ways that mirror God's care for justice, mercy, and integrity.

This means:

- The gift of being set right leads into a **life of doing what is right**.

- Personal morality and **social justice** both belong under tsedaqah/dikaiosynē.

- Righteousness is both **status** and **pattern**, both **position** and **practice**.

To be righteous, biblically, is to be a person whose **relationships, choices, and structures** are being brought into alignment with God's character.

5. How our language splits what Scripture joins

English tends to split:

- **"Righteousness"** – private, spiritual, vertical (me and God).

- **"Justice"** – public, social, horizontal (society and courts).

The biblical words do not draw a hard line there.

- Tsedaqah/dikaiosynē is **relational** in all directions: toward God, neighbor, community, and creation.

- To be "righteous" is to **treat others rightly**, not just to have right beliefs.

- To do "justice" is to **embody God's righteousness** in practical care for others, especially the vulnerable.

If we hear "righteousness" only as my private holiness, we may ignore **systemic injustice** and material needs. If we hear "justice" only as social activism, we may ignore **personal repentance, worship, and holiness**.

Scripture's vocabulary insists that both belong together.

6. What did it say first—and how can we hear it now?

If we listen to these words in their own world:

- **Tsedaqah** first said: **rightness**—straightness, integrity, justice, generosity expressed in real relationships and structures.

- **Dikaiosynē** said: **righteousness/justice**—being in the right and doing what is right according to God's standard, both in personal and communal life.

For us, that means:

- When we read "righteousness," we can also hear **"God-shaped justice in relationships and society."**

- When we read "justice," we can also hear **"living out God's righteousness, not just human fairness."**

- When we talk about being "right with God," we can expect that rightness to **spill over** into how we treat others.

In the storyline of this book:

- Grace is God's **free favor**.

- Faith is our **trusting loyalty**.

- Righteousness/justice is the **set-right life** that grace and faith are meant to produce—a life where God's character is reflected in **both inner integrity and outward fairness**.

7. Try it yourself

Here are some ways to let tsedaqah and dikaiosynē deepen your understanding:

1. **Read a "justice and righteousness" pairing**

- Find a verse where both appear together.

- Paraphrase them as "setting things right" and "living rightly."

- Ask: What would this look like in my town, my church, my home?

1. **Track "righteousness of God" in one New Testament passage**

- Read a section where the phrase appears.

- Ask: Where is it describing God's **character**, where His **saving action**, and where the **status and life** of His people?

- Notice how all three hang together.

1. **Name one "set-right" step**

- Identify an area—personal or communal—where things are **crooked**.

- Ask: What small act could participate in God's tsedaqah/dikaiosynē here—telling the truth, making restitution, advocating, giving, reconciling?

- See that step as part of the **righteousness and justice** God delights in.

As you practice, "righteousness" and "justice" will sound less like two warring agendas and more like what they were from the beginning: **one call to live in right relationship with the God who sets things right.**

Part V

Time, Judgement, Law, and "Hell"

Books by Rene'

Chapter 23

Ages and "Forever"

'Olam, Aiōn, Aiōnios

When English Bibles say **"forever," "eternal,"** or **"everlasting,"** they are usually translating the Hebrew **'olam** or the Greek **aiōn / aiōnios**. Our ears often hear these as simple words for **endless time**. In Scripture, they start with a more flexible idea: an **age**, a **long duration**, or something that belongs to **God's own kind of time**. This chapter asks: what did 'olam, aiōn, and aiōnios say first? And how can that help us hear passages about "eternal life" and "eternal punishment" more carefully?

1. 'Olam in the Old Testament: long duration, hidden horizon

The Hebrew noun **'olam** ( )□□□□□□appears hundreds of times. Lexicons summarize it as:

- **Long duration, antiquity, futurity**.

- A time "to the distant horizon," sometimes past, sometimes future.

- Often rendered "forever," "everlasting," "of old," "for a long time."

Key points:

- 'Olam can look **backward** – "of old," "from ancient times."

- It can look **forward** – "for ever," "to all generations."

- Sometimes context explicitly **limits** it (for example, "forever" for the life of a servant, or for as long as a temple stands).

So 'olam by itself does not always mean "endless in the modern mathematical sense." It means:

- **As far as you can see** in a given direction.

- The whole span of an **age or order**, whether that is a person's life, a dynasty, a covenant, or God's own reign.

When 'olam describes God—His love, His covenant, His kingdom—it points to **unbounded faithfulness**: His rule is not like a human king's reign that comes and goes. When it describes created arrangements, it can mean **age-long**, lasting as long as that order of things.

2. Aiōn in the New Testament: age, world, and beyond

The Greek noun **aiōn** (αἰών) is the usual equivalent of 'olam in the Greek Old Testament and in the New Testament. Lexicons gloss it as:

- **Age, era, time-span.**

- By extension, the **world** as arranged in a particular age.

- Sometimes, **eternity**—especially when multiplied ("unto the ages of the ages").

The New Testament uses aiōn in several ways:

- "This **age**" versus "the **age** to come" – two orders of reality and history.

- "The **course** of this world" – the pattern of life in the present age.

- "Forever and ever" – literally "unto the ages of the ages," a way of piling up ages to express **unbounded duration**.

So aiōn keeps the **"age"** meaning at its core. Whether it points to a limited era or to what we call "forever" depends on:

- What is being described (God's life, Christ's kingdom, human arrangements).

- How the phrase is built (single "age" vs. "ages of ages").

3. Aiōnios: of the age, belonging to God's forever

The adjective **aiōnios** (αἰώνιος) is usually translated **"eternal"** or **"everlasting."** Etymologically it means:

- **"Of an age"** or "age-long."

- Belonging to the **coming age**, especially in Jewish and Christian usage.

Lexicons and usage show:

- When aiōnios describes **God**, His **life**, His kingdom, and His glory, it clearly points to what has **no end**.

- When it describes **"eternal life,"** it means both:

- Life of the **coming age**, and

- Life that is **unending** because it is God's own kind of life shared with us.

- When it describes **"eternal punishment"** or **"eternal fire,"** it likewise points to something with **enduring, age-defining seriousness**—though Christians have long debated the precise nature and duration.

The key is that aiōnios emphasizes **quality and belonging** as well as duration:

- It is **age-of-God** life, judgment, or glory—rooted in God's own life, not just in the clock.

4. This age and the age to come

Across the Bible, particularly in Jewish Second Temple thought and the New Testament, history is often seen in terms of **two ages**:

- **This present age** – marked by sin, death, injustice, and the powers opposed to God.

- **The age to come** – marked by God's rule made manifest, resurrection, justice, and peace.

Within that framework:

- "Eternal life" is literally **"life of the age"**—the life of the **age to come**, already tasted now in Christ.

- "Eternal punishment" is judgment that belongs to that same **decisive age**.

- When Jesus speaks of sins that "will not be forgiven, either in this age or in the age to come," He is using the same two-age framework.

This helps us see:

- Salvation is not only about **escaping this world** but about **entering the life of the new age** here and now, to be completed in the resurrection.

- Judgment is not only about **time length**, but about **final seriousness**—decisions that belong to the climactic age of God's rule.

5. How "forever" and "eternity" can mislead us

Our English words "forever," "eternal," and "eternity" tend to sound purely **mathematical**:

- A line with no end.

- Endless extension of the same kind of time we know.

Biblical language is more **storied and relational**:

- ʻOlam and aiōn focus on **ages**, orders of reality, and long spans, not on abstract endlessness.

- Aiōnios focuses on what **belongs to God's age**—His enduring reign, His kind of life.

Two dangers:

1. **Shrinking "eternal life"**

- If we hear only "never-ending time in heaven," we may miss that eternal life begins **now**, as participation in God's own life through Christ and the Spirit.

- The focus in many passages is **knowing God**, sharing His life, and bearing the life of the coming age into the present.

1. **Debating only timelines for judgment**

- Passages about "eternal punishment" have been read in different ways within Christian history.

- Without settling those debates here, we can say: aiōnios certainly marks out **the seriousness and age-defining weight** of God's judgment.

- Reducing everything to a question of "how many minutes on the clock" can miss the point that Scripture is calling us, above all, to **reverent seriousness and urgent response**.

6. What did it say first—and how can we hear it now?

Listening back:

- **'Olam** said: **long, hidden horizon**—a duration whose ends we do not see clearly; an age, sometimes effectively "forever" when applied to God and His ultimate purposes.

- **Aiōn** said: **age, era, world order**, sometimes extended to "ages of ages" to express unbounded duration.

- **Aiōnios** said: **age-of-God**, belonging to the age of God's reign—life, joy, glory, or judgment rooted in His own enduring reality.

For us, that means:

- When we see "eternal life," we can think: **"the life of God's coming age, starting now and never ending"**, not only "life after death."

- When we see "eternal" attached to God, we can hear: **"beyond and above all ages, faithful without end."**

- When we see "forever" or "everlasting," we can remember to ask:

- Is this describing **God and His final kingdom** (unending), or

- A **long, age-long arrangement** within the story (long but not ultimate)?

This keeps us anchored in what the Bible is doing with time: telling the story of **ages** and **the God who holds them**, rather than giving us a bare vocabulary lesson in infinity.

7. Try it yourself

Here are a few ways to let ʿolam, aiōn, and aiōnios sharpen your reading:

1. **Mark "this age / age to come" texts**

- Find several passages that use that contrast.

- Ask: How does this two-age picture change how I understand "eternal life" and "world" language?

1. **Re-read a key "eternal life" verse with "life of the age"**

- Paraphrase: "whoever believes has **the life of God's coming age**."

- Reflect: What does that say about your life **now**, not just after death?

1. **Notice different uses of "forever" in the Old Testament**

- Compare where "forever" clearly describes God's own reign with where it describes more limited arrangements.

- Let that variety remind you to read ʿolam in context.

As you do, "forever" and "eternal" will begin to sound less flat and more like what Scripture meant from the beginning: language for **ages and horizons** under the care of the God whose faithfulness, love, and kingdom truly **have no end**.

Chapter 24

Days and Seasons

Mo ed and Kairos

We measure time with clocks and calendars: seconds, hours, weeks, fiscal quarters. Scripture uses ordinary time words too, but it also has special terms for **God-appointed times**—moments and seasons when He chooses to meet, act, or call for a response. In the Old Testament, one key word is **mo'ed**. In the New Testament, a key counterpart is **kairos**. Both point beyond "time in general" to **time on purpose**.

This chapter asks: What did **mo'ed** and **kairos** say first? How do they shape Israel's calendar and the church's sense of God's timing, and how do our flat words "time" and "season" sometimes hide the sense of **appointment**?

1. Mo'ed in the Old Testament: God's appointments

The Hebrew word **mo'ed** ( )□□□□□□□can mean:

- **Appointed time** – a set date or season.

- **Meeting** – a scheduled gathering.

- **Appointed place** – especially where God meets His people.

- By extension, **appointed festivals**.

In Israel's Scriptures, mo'ed is used for:

- The **tent of meeting** – the place of encounter.

- The **weekly Sabbath** – a recurring appointed time of rest and worship.

- The **festivals** (mo'edim) – Passover, Weeks, Booths, and others, God's "appointed times" in the year.

Mo'edim are not just days off or cultural holidays. They are **appointments set by God**:

- Times to **remember** His saving acts.

- Times to **rehearse** the story of rescue and covenant.

- Times to **meet** with Him as a people.

Israel's calendar is thus not just agricultural or political; it is **theological**. Time itself is structured around **meeting God**.

2. Mo'ed: place, calendar, and story

Uses of mo'ed cluster in three spheres:

- **Place** – the "tent of mo'ed," where God's presence dwells and where He speaks.

- **Calendar** – the yearly cycle of mo'edim, God's appointed feasts and holy days.

- **Story moments** – specific times God appoints for judgment, deliverance, or visitation.

This means:

- Time is not neutral or empty; it is a **stage** where God has set certain key appointments.

- The people of God are called to **order their days and years** around His schedule, not only their own.

- Remembering and keeping the moʿedim teaches each generation **who God is** and **what He has done.**

When we see "appointed time" or "festivals" in English, we are often hearing moʿed behind it—God's **calendar of encounter.**

3. Kairos in the New Testament: the right, appointed time

Greek has more than one word for time. Two important ones are:

- **Chronos** – time as **duration**, the ongoing flow of moments ("hours," "years").

- **Kairos** – time as **occasion**, the **right time**, a **decisive moment.**

Lexicons summarize **kairos** as:

- **Set time, season, opportunity, fitting moment.**

- Not how long something lasts, but **what kind of time** it is—a time ripe for something.

The New Testament uses kairos for:

- Agricultural imagery – "a season" for sowing or harvest.

- Life stages and **opportune moments.**

- Crucial **points in salvation history**, especially around Christ's coming, death, and resurrection.

- The **"right time"** for God's action and our response.

Where chronos answers "how long?", kairos answers **"what time is this, in God's purposes?"**

4. "The time is fulfilled": kairos and the kingdom

When Jesus begins His public ministry, He announces:

"The time (kairos) is fulfilled, and the kingdom of God is at hand; repent and believe in the gospel."

Here:

- "The **kairos** is fulfilled" – the **appointed moment** in God's story-line has arrived.

- The kingdom's nearness is not a vague idea; it is a **present opportunity** demanding response.

Elsewhere, kairos marks:

- "The **proper time**" for Christ's death and resurrection.

- "The **right season**" for bearing certain fruits or performing certain ministries.

- "An **acceptable time**" or "day of salvation" in which God's grace is offered.

Kairos thus carries the same sense of **appointment** we saw in mo'ed, now centered on Christ and the unfolding of the gospel.

5. Days and seasons: living in God's time

The Bible's time words help us see two layers:

- **Ordinary time** – days, months, years (chronos), the rhythms of work and rest.

- **Appointed time** – mo'ed and kairos, moments and seasons where God's purposes come into particular focus.

For Israel:

- Weekly Sabbaths and yearly festivals **sanctified** the calendar.

- Certain historical moments—exodus, exile, return—became mo'ed points of reference.

For the church:

- The **coming of Christ** marks the central kairos in history.

- Believers are urged to "redeem the time (kairos)"—to recognize and use the opportunities God gives.

- Certain seasons (suffering, proclamation, growth, danger) are treated as **charged times** requiring particular faithfulness.

Living wisely means:

- Not only counting days, but **discerning seasons**.

- Asking, in any stretch of time: "What kind of time is this, in God's story? What response is fitting now?"

6. How our language flattens "time" and "season"

In English, "time" and "season" can sound generic.

- "Time" often just means "clock time"—hours available, schedule space.

- "Season" may mean a vague life phase or a cultural period ("holiday season") without reference to God.

Compared to mo'ed and kairos, this is thin. Biblical language suggests:

- Some times are **appointed**—not in the sense that we can decode every detail, but in the sense that God **really does act** at particular moments.

- Our calendars and rhythms can be shaped to **remember and meet Him**, not just to chase productivity or leisure.

- Opportunities to repent, to serve, to speak, or to rest are **salient moments**, not random.

If we flatten everything into generic time, we may miss the weight of **"now"** in Scripture.

7. What did it say first—and how can we hear it now?

Listening back:

- **Mo'ed** said: **appointed time, meeting, festival**—a God-set occasion to gather, remember, and encounter Him.

- **Kairos** said: **fitting, appointed moment or season**—a time charged with significance in God's plan, inviting decisive response.

For us, that means:

- When we see "appointed time" in our Old Testaments, we can think **"God's appointment with His people,"** not just "date on a calendar."

- When we hear Jesus say "the time is fulfilled," we can hear **"the**

long-awaited moment has arrived—act now.”

- When we are told to "redeem the time," we can think **"make the most of the kairos God gives"**, not just "be efficient."

Time, in Scripture, is not just something we **use**; it is something God **fills** with His presence and purposes.

8. Try it yourself

Here are some simple ways to let mo'ed and kairos reshape your sense of time:

1. **Read a festival passage with "appointment" in mind**

- Take a section like Leviticus 23.

- Each time you see "feast" or "appointed time," think "God's scheduled appointment with His people."

- Ask: What does this reveal about how God wants to shape Israel's year?

1. **Mark kairos uses in one New Testament book**

- Choose a Gospel or letter and underline "time/season" where the underlying word is kairos.

- Ask: What kind of moment is this? What response is being called for?

1. **Name one "kairos moment" in your current life**

- Reflect: Is there a particular opportunity, challenge, or call that makes **this** a charged season?

- Pray: "Teach me to recognize this as a mo'ed/kairos with You, and to respond in the way that fits what You're doing."

As you practice, "time" will begin to sound less like a neutral backdrop and more like what Scripture portrays: **a tapestry of days and seasons in which God sets appointments, opens windows, and invites His people to trust, remember, and act.**

Chapter 25

Sheol, Hades, Gehenna, Tartarus

What We Call "Hell"

When English Bibles say **"hell,"** they are usually translating not one but several different words: **Sheol, Hades, Gehenna,** and **Tartarus.** We often hear "hell" and picture one final place of fiery punishment. Scripture's vocabulary is more varied. It talks about the **realm of the dead,** a **valley of judgment,** and even a **prison for rebellious angels.** This chapter asks: what did each of these words say first, and how does flattening them into one word distort what the Bible is doing?

1. Sheol: the shadowy underworld in the Hebrew Bible

The Hebrew word **Sheol** ( )שׁאוֹל is the main Old Testament term for the **realm of the dead**.

Key features:

- It is pictured as **down below**—a pit, depths, underworld.

- It is associated with **darkness, silence, and forgetfulness.**

- Both **righteous and wicked** are said to go there, at least in many texts.

Sometimes Sheol overlaps with the idea of **"grave"**—where a person ends up when they die. In other passages, it seems like a more developed **underworld**:

- The dead are gathered there as "shades."

- They are cut off from the visible presence of God and from human society.

- There is a sense of **loss and diminished existence**, not yet a clear picture of final heaven or hell.

Sheol is often **neutral in tone**: it is where you go when you die, not yet a fully defined place of reward or punishment. Yet:

- God is still **Lord over Sheol**—He can bring down to it and **raise up** from it.

- Some texts express hope that God will not abandon His faithful ones there.

2. Hades: the Greek Sheol and more

The Greek word **Hades** (ᾅδης) is the usual New Testament counterpart to Sheol.

Its basic sense:

- The **abode of the dead**.

- The **unseen world** where the departed go.

In the Greek Old Testament, Hades often translates **Sheol**, keeping the sense of **underworld**. In the New Testament:

- Hades can simply mean the **realm of the dead** (for example, in quotations from Psalms about not being left in Hades).

- In some passages, it has a sharper edge, associated with **torment** for the wicked while they await final judgment.

Jesus' story of the rich man and Lazarus, for example, depicts:

- The rich man in **Hades**, in torment.

- A great chasm between him and the comfort of Abraham's side.

Here Hades functions more like an **intermediate state**: a temporary realm of the dead where destinies are already distinguished, even before the final resurrection and judgment.

So:

- **Sheol / Hades** together speak of the **realm of the dead**.

- Sometimes the focus is simply "the place of the dead."

- Sometimes the focus is on **conscious experience—comfort or torment—before the final day.**

3. Gehenna: from Jerusalem's valley to final judgment

Gehenna (γέεννα) is the Greek form of the Hebrew phrase **Ge Hinnom**, the **Valley of Hinnom** just outside Jerusalem.

Historically:

- This valley was associated with **idolatry and child sacrifice**, where some kings burned their sons as offerings to foreign gods.

- Prophets condemned these practices and declared that the valley would become a place of **judgment and disgrace**, where corpses would be thrown.

Over time, the Hinnom Valley became:

- A symbol of **shameful destruction**.

- In some traditions, a **garbage and refuse site**—dirty, smoldering, and defiled.

- A vivid picture of **what it looks like when God's judgment falls**.

When Jesus warns about being thrown into **Gehenna**, English Bibles often render it "hell." In His teaching:

- Gehenna is associated with **fire, destruction**, and being **cast out**.

- It is used as an image for **final, decisive judgment**, especially for those who persist in leading others astray or clinging to hypocrisy and violence.

Important:

- Gehenna is not a generic mythological underworld; it is a **specific valley with a history** in Israel's story.

- Jesus takes this notorious place and uses it as a **living metaphor** for the seriousness of God's judgment on unrepentant evil.

4. Tartarus: a prison for rebellious angels

The word **Tartarus** does not appear as a noun in the New Testament, but a verb derived from it appears once, in 2 Peter.

- In Greek mythology, **Tartarus** was the **lowest part of the underworld**, a deep abyss where rebellious gods or giants were imprisoned.

- The verb used in 2 Peter means "to **cast into Tartarus**."

In that verse:

- God is said not to have spared **angels who sinned**, but to have

cast them into Tartarus, keeping them in gloomy chains until judgment.

So:

- Tartarus is portrayed as a **holding place for rebellious angels**, not primarily for humans.

- It functions as an image of **deep, dark confinement** under God's authority.

This usage is unique, and we should be cautious about building a detailed geography from it. It adds a piece to the picture: Scripture can borrow familiar cultural language (here, a Greek term) to describe **divine punishment of spiritual beings**.

5. Why one English "hell" can be misleading

English translations sometimes use "hell" for:

- Sheol

- Hades

- Gehenna

- Tartarus

When we read "hell," we may imagine:

- A single, final place of **eternal conscious torment** after judgment.

But the biblical vocabulary distinguishes:

- The **realm of the dead** (Sheol/Hades), which can be neutral or, in later usage, divided between comfort and torment.

- A **symbolic valley** turned into an image of **final judgment** (Gehenna).

- A **prison for angels** (Tartarus).

Flattening all these into "hell" can:

- Merge the **intermediate state** (before final judgment) and the **final outcome** in ways Scripture does not always do.

- Hide the **Jewish and geographical roots** of Gehenna.

- Make it harder to follow the **development** of ideas about death, judgment, and afterlife across the Bible.

Recognizing the differences does not settle every theological debate about the nature or duration of final judgment. It simply lets each word contribute its own piece to the picture.

6. What did they say first—and how can we hear them now?

Summing up:

- **Sheol** – the Old Testament **underworld / realm of the dead**, often shadowy and neutral, where all the dead go, yet still under God's power.

- **Hades** – the Greek term for the realm of the dead, used in the New Testament for that same idea, sometimes with a focus on **torment for the wicked** before final judgment.

- **Gehenna** – the **Valley of Hinnom**, a real place of past atrocities and prophetic warnings, taken up by Jesus as a vivid symbol of **God's final judgment** on evil.

- **Tartarus** – a term applied to the **imprisonment of rebellious angels**, a deep, dark holding place until judgment.

For us, that means:

- When we read "hell," it is worth asking: **which word is underneath?** Are we hearing about the general realm of the dead, a warning image of final judgment, or something else?

- When we think about judgment, we can be more attentive to the **story-shaped images** Scripture uses, rather than importing a single, flattened picture.

- When we talk about the gospel as "salvation from hell," we can remember that Scripture presents salvation positively as **sharing in God's life and kingdom**, and negatively as rescue from **sin, death, and the various forms of separation from God** that these words point to.

Taken together, Sheol, Hades, Gehenna, and Tartarus do not give us a neat map of the afterlife. They do something more important: they **insist** that our lives are lived before a God who takes evil seriously, holds the dead in His hand, and will ultimately **set things right**—for justice, for mercy, and for the renewal of all things.

In Scripture, these four terms are related but distinct.

- **Sheol** (Hebrew) is the Old Testament term for the **realm of the dead**, pictured as a shadowy underworld "down below." Both righteous and wicked go there; it can overlap with "the grave," but also evokes a silent, diminished existence awaiting God's action.

- **Hades** (Greek) is the New Testament counterpart to Sheol: the **state or place of the dead**. It can mean simply "the grave" or disembodied existence (even Jesus is said to have been in Hades in the sense of being among the dead), and in some passages it refers more specifically to the **temporary abode of the wicked dead in torment** before final judgment.

- **Gehenna** is Greek for the **Valley of Hinnom** outside Jerusalem, a real valley where some kings practiced child sacrifice and where prophetic oracles pictured corpses piled in judgment. By Jesus' day, this valley symbolized **fiery judgment**; Jesus uses "Gehenna" as a vivid image for God's final, unquenchable judgment on evil, and English Bibles often render it "hell."

- **Tartarus** appears as a verb once in 2 Peter 2:4, drawn from Greek mythology where Tartarus is the deepest part of the underworld. Peter uses it to describe God **casting sinful angels into a dark prison** to be held until judgment; it is a place for rebellious angels, not described as the final destination of humans.

So:

- Sheol/Hades = **realm of the dead**, an intermediate state under God's control.

- Gehenna = **image of final judgment**, rooted in a specific valley and Israel's history.

- Tartarus = **angelic prison** for certain rebellious spirits until the great day.

When English translations use "hell" for more than one of these, it can blur differences between the **general underworld**, the **symbolic picture of final punishment**, and the **confinement of angels**.

Judgment and Justice

Mishpat and Krisis

In everyday speech, **"judgment"** often sounds like harsh criticism or a final negative verdict. In Scripture, the main words for judgment—**mishpat** in Hebrew and **krisis** in Greek—are wider and more hopeful. They name God's work of **weighing, sorting, and setting things right**. Judgment can be terrifying for unrepentant evil, but it is also good news for victims, the oppressed, and all who long for truth.

This chapter asks: What did **mishpat** and **krisis** say first? How do they relate to righteousness and justice, and how does a thin English "judgment" miss both their severity and their hope?

1. Mishpat in the Old Testament: decisions that set things right

The Hebrew noun **mishpat** ( )□□□□□□□□□□comes from a root meaning **to judge, to govern**. Word studies summarize mishpat as:

- **Judgment, decision, verdict** – the ruling of a judge.

- **Justice, legal right** – the order that flows from right judgments.

- **Ordinance, law** – the rulings and regulations that embody God's standards.

Mishpat appears in several overlapping ways:

- **Act of judging** – deciding a case, distinguishing right from wrong.

- **Outcome** – the **verdict** or **sentence** pronounced.

- **System** – the structures (courts, procedures) that apply justice.

- **Attribute** – God's own **justice** and His way of ruling.

In Israel:

- Judges are to **"do mishpat"**—hear cases fairly, protect the weak, restrain the strong.

- The people are commanded to keep God's **"judgments"**—His mishpatim—as part of the covenant.

- Prophets condemn those who **twist mishpat**, who pervert justice for bribes or neglect the cause of the vulnerable.

Mishpat is thus both **process** and **result**: the doing of justice and the just order that results.

2. Judgment as good news: God the Judge

The Old Testament repeatedly celebrates God as **Judge**:

- "He has established His throne for judgment; He judges the world with righteousness."

- "All His ways are mishpat."

This means:

- God's judgments are **fair and faithful**—no bribe, bias, or ignorance.

- His great acts in history (flood, exodus, exile, return) are seen as **judgments**—decisions to confront evil and defend the oppressed.

- Future hope includes a day when God will **judge the nations** with justice, ending oppression.

For victims and the faithful:

- Mishpat is **comfort**: wrongs will not stand forever.

- Judgment is **rescue**: God's verdict against oppressors is at the same time His **vindication** of the wronged.

So biblical judgment is not just about **punishment**; it is about **setting things right**.

3. Krisis in the New Testament: decision, separation, and the last day

The Greek noun **krisis** (κρίσις) and related verb **krinō** mean:

- **Judgment, decision, verdict.**

- A **trial**, the process of weighing a case.

- A **separation**—sorting out.

Krisis is used for:

- **Present judgment** – people's response to Jesus brings a kind of judgment on themselves.

- **Individual judgment** – God's decisions about right and wrong in a person's life.

- **Future, final judgment** – the "day of judgment," when God will judge the living and the dead.

Key themes:

- There is an **appointed time** when all will give account.

- Christ is central in this krisis—He is the one through whom God judges and saves.

- Rejecting the light brings krisis now; the final day will confirm and unveil that decision.

Krisis includes both:

- **Condemnation** for persistent evil.

- **Vindication** for those who belong to Christ.

4. Judgment, righteousness, and mercy woven together

Mishpat and krisis are closely tied to the words we saw in the last chapter:

- **Tsedaqah / dikaiosynē** – righteousness/justice.

- **Mishpat / krisis** – judgment, the act of deciding and enforcing what is right.

Together they show:

- God's **character** – He is righteous and just.

- God's **action** – He judges (does mishpat), making decisions that uphold righteousness.

- God's **mercy** – He provides ways for sinners to be rightly judged yet **rescued** (sacrifice in the Old Testament; Christ's cross in the New).

In the cross:

- God's **judgment on sin** is revealed—sin is not ignored or excused.

- God's **justifying mercy** is revealed—those in Christ are declared in the right, not because they have none of their own sin, but because Christ has borne judgment for them.

So when the New Testament speaks of "no krisis" for those who believe, it means:

- They do not face the **condemning verdict**; their judgment has been borne and resolved in Christ.

- They still live under God's discerning eye and fatherly discipline, but not under His wrath.

5. How our language flattens "judgment"

Our word "judgment" can flatten mishpat and krisis in several ways.

- It may sound purely **negative**—only about condemnation, not about vindication or restoration.

- It may sound purely **future**, as if God is not judging now in ways that confront and expose evil.

- It may sound purely **individual**, ignoring God's judgments on **systems, nations, and histories**.

Biblically:

- Judgment includes both **punishing wrong** and **defending the wronged**.

- God's acts in history can be called judgments (on empires, idols, unjust practices).

- The final judgment is both **warning** and **hope**: evil will not have the last word.

If we think of judgment only as God "zapping people," we may miss:

- That His judgments are also **acts of love** for those harmed by evil.

- That His call to repentance is a mercy meant to **change the verdict**.

- That His ultimate goal is a world where **justice and peace** meet.

6. What did it say first—and how can we hear it now?

Listening back:

- **Mishpat** first said: **judgment/justice**—the act of deciding cases, the verdicts given, and the just order God intends for society.

- **Krisis** said: **decision, judgment, separation**—the weighing and deciding that reveals what is right and brings consequences.

For us, that means:

- When we read "judgment," we can think: **"God's truthful decision that sets things right,"** not only "God being mad."

- When we contemplate the "day of judgment," we can hold together **sobriety** (evil will be exposed and condemned) and **hope** (wrongs will be righted, the faithful vindicated).

- When we hear the gospel, we can see it as God's **great act of judgment** in which He condemns sin in Christ and opens a way for sinners to stand in the right.

In the flow of this part of the book:

- Sin terms (chata', avon, anomia) named our **misdirection and rebellion**.

- Peace and salvation terms (shalom, yasha', sōzō) named God's **healing and rescue**.

- Judgment terms (mishpat, krisis) name the **truthful, decisive acts** by which God deals with both, so that His world can finally reflect His righteousness and His love.

7. Try it yourself

Here are a few ways to let mishpat and krisis reshape your view of judgment:

1. **Read a "judgment psalm" with victims in mind**

- Take a psalm that celebrates God's judgment.

- Ask: For whom is this **good news**? Who is being defended, not just punished?

1. **Trace judgment language in a Gospel passage**

- In a section where Jesus speaks of judgment, note where krisis or related terms appear.

- Ask: How does Jesus' coming **bring judgment now**, not only later?

1. **Name one area needing mishpat in your world**

- Identify a situation (personal, local, global) where justice is distorted.

- Pray for God's mishpat there—and ask how you might participate, in small ways, in **aligning with His just decisions**.

As you do, "judgment" may begin to sound less like a one-note threat and more like what Scripture has always meant: the **clear-eyed, truth-telling, world-setting-right** work of the God who refuses to leave evil unaddressed or the oppressed unheard.

Chapter 27

Torah and Law

Instruction vs Rulebook

Many English readers hear **"law"** and imagine a thick rulebook: regulations to keep so we do not get in trouble. When the Bible speaks of **Torah**, it can include commands, but its primary flavor is **teaching, guidance, and story-shaped instruction**. Torah is God **showing a people how to live** in light of who He is and what He has done, not just handing them a legal code to comply with.

This chapter asks: What did "Torah" say first? How did it get translated as "law"? And what do we lose when "law" sounds like a cold rulebook instead of a Father teaching children how to walk?

1. What "Torah" means: pointing the way

The Hebrew word **Torah** comes from a verb that means **to teach, to point out, to instruct**. In the Old Testament it can mean:

- Specific **instructions or rulings** given for a situation.

- The broader **teaching** given through Moses.

- Eventually, the **first five books** themselves (Genesis–Deuteronomy) as "the Torah of Moses."

So Torah is:

- God's **instructional guidance** for His people.

- Rooted not just in commands, but in **story**—creation, exodus, covenant.

- Given in a **relational context**: the God who rescued Israel from slavery now teaches them how to live in freedom.

If you ask, "What is Torah?" the answer is not just "rules," but "the whole **instructional package** by which God forms a people."

2. Torah as story-framed instruction, not bare code

The shape of the Torah itself makes this clear.

- Genesis is mostly **narrative**: it tells where Israel came from, who their God is, and what went wrong with the world.

- Exodus mixes narrative and command: God **rescues** first, then gives covenant instructions at Sinai.

- Leviticus and Numbers blend laws with stories of failure and mercy in the wilderness.

- Deuteronomy is sermon-like **re-teaching** for a new generation on the edge of the land.

That means:

- Commands are embedded in a **story of grace**. God does not start with "Do this"; He starts with "I brought you out."

- The instructions are given to shape a **way of life**—worship, justice, family, economics—not just to regulate ritual details.

- Even the more technical parts (sacrifices, purity, festivals) are woven into a picture of **God dwelling with His people**.

Torah is more like a parent patiently training a family over time than a bureaucrat issuing a list of regulations.

3. From Torah to "nomos": what happens in Greek

When the Hebrew Bible was translated into Greek (the Septuagint), Torah was usually rendered by **nomos**, the Greek word for **law**.

Nomos could mean:

- Law in a legal sense.

- Custom, norm, shared way of life.

By the time of the New Testament:

- "The Law" (ho nomos) often referred broadly to **Torah**, sometimes specifically to the books of Moses, sometimes to the legal commandments within them.

- "Law and Prophets" became a shorthand for the **Scriptures**.

So when Paul and others speak about **nomos**, they are:

- Often talking about **Torah as a covenant framework** for Israel.

- Sometimes focusing on specific **commandments** (circumcision, food laws, Sabbath markers).

- Sometimes using "law" in a more **universal sense** (a law written on the heart, a principle at work in members, and so on).

The shift from "instruction" to "law" is not wrong, but it is **narrower**. It tilts us toward hearing rules, not relational teaching.

4. Law in Paul: gift, tutor, and limit

Paul's letters wrestle deeply with **Torah / nomos** now that Messiah has come.

He can say very positive things:

- The law is **holy, righteous, and good**.

- The law was a kind of **guardian or tutor**, leading God's people up to Christ.

- The law revealed **God's will** and exposed sin.

He can also speak of its limitations:

- The law, by itself, cannot **give the life** it describes; it tells what is right but does not change the heart.

- The law can become a **badge of boundary-marking** (who is in or out) rather than a channel of welcome.

- Under sin's power, the good law can be twisted into a tool for **boasting or despair**.

For Paul, the solution is not to treat Torah as a failed rulebook, but to see it as **fulfilled and re-read in Christ**:

- Jesus embodies the **true meaning of the law**—love of God and neighbor in a Spirit-empowered life.

- Believers are no longer "under law" as a condemning covenant, but **under grace**, receiving the Spirit who writes God's instruction on their hearts.

- The law's **core instruction** (love) is now written within, not just on stone or page.

If we hear only "law vs grace," we miss that grace is God's way of finally **making His Torah take root** inside His people.

5. Instruction vs rulebook: how flattening changes our hearing

When "Torah" is flattened to "law" in the rulebook sense, several distortions creep in.

- We may imagine God's primary posture as **policing**, not **parenting**—as if He mostly watches for infractions instead of teaching us to flourish.

- We may reduce the Old Testament to **obsolete regulations**, ignoring its rich story and wisdom as ongoing instruction about God's character and priorities.

- We may misread Paul as rejecting the entire Old Testament, rather than critiquing a **particular way** of clinging to Torah apart from Christ and the Spirit.

Recovering Torah as **instruction** helps us see:

- Continuity: God has **always** been about forming a people who reflect His character.

- Fulfillment: Jesus does not throw away God's instruction; He **embodies and deepens** it, especially in His teaching on love, mercy, and justice.

- Transformation: The Spirit does not free us from listening to God's instruction; He **enables** us to live it from the inside out.

Instead of asking, "Which rules still apply?" we can begin with, "What is God **teaching** here about who He is and how His people are to live?" Then we discern how that instruction is taken up, intensified, or re-expressed in Christ.

6. What did it say first—and how can we hear it now?

Listening back:

- **Torah** first said: **instruction, teaching, guidance**—God pointing the way for a rescued people to live well with Him and with each other.

- **Nomos / law** highlighted the **command and covenant** side of that instruction, but can sound too thin and legalistic if we forget the story and relationship behind it.

For us, that means:

- When you see "law" in your Bible, pause and ask: "Is this talking about **Torah as God's whole instruction** to His people, or a specific set of commands?"

- When you read Torah itself, look for the **teacher's heart**—how God uses story, promise, warning, and concrete practices to shape a community.

- When you read Paul on law, remember that his problem is not with God's instruction, but with any attempt to **be right with God by the rulebook alone**, without the gift of Christ and the Spirit.

Seeing Torah as instruction rather than mere rulebook does not make God's commands optional. It does something harder and better: it invites us to receive His words as the **wise, loving training** of the One who rescued us—and who now patiently teaches us how to walk.

Chapter 28

Covenant and Testament

Berit and Diathēkē

When we open a Bible, the page often says "Old Testament" and "New Testament." Behind that word "testament" stand two rich terms: **berit** in Hebrew and **diathēkē** in Greek. Both are usually translated **"covenant"**—not just a contract, but a binding, relational commitment in which God ties His own name to a people and a future.

This chapter asks: What did **berit** and **diathēkē** say first? How did "testament" become the label for our two-part Bible? And how does seeing **covenant** instead of just "old vs new" change how we read?

1. Berit: God's binding, relational commitment

The Hebrew word **berit** (often spelled berith/beriyth) is the main Old Testament term for **covenant**.

At its core, berit means:

- A **solemn, binding agreement** between parties.

- Often ratified by **oaths, signs, and sometimes sacrifice.**

- Carrying **promises, obligations, and consequences.**

In Scripture, berit appears in several key relationships:

- **Noah**: God promises never again to destroy all flesh with a flood, setting the rainbow as a sign. This is a **cosmic covenant** of preservation.

- **Abraham**: God binds Himself to Abraham and his descendants—to bless them, give land, and bless all nations through them. This is a **family-to-nations covenant**.

- **Sinai (Moses)**: After the exodus, God makes a covenant with Israel as a nation, giving Torah as **the covenant's way of life**.

- **David**: God promises David a lasting dynasty—a **royal covenant** focused on a king.

- **New covenant promises** in the prophets: God speaks of an **everlasting covenant**, writing His instruction on hearts and forgiving iniquity.

Key features of berit:

- It is deeply **relational**—about belonging, loyalty, and identity.

- It is often **initiated by God**; Israel is called to respond in faith and obedience.

- It has an **"if / then"** dimension (blessings and curses) especially in the Mosaic covenant, but underneath that lies God's **steadfast commitment** to His own promises.

So berit is not just a deal; it is God saying, "I will be your God, and you will be My people," and then binding Himself to that word.

2. Diathēkē: covenant, and also "testament"

In the Greek Old Testament (Septuagint), berit is almost always translated

diathēkē.

In wider Greek usage, diathēkē can mean:

- A **formal arrangement or disposition** of benefits.

- Especially a **last will and testament**—a declaration of how benefits will be distributed after death.

In the Bible:

- Diathēkē is used to carry over the full weight of **berit**—God's covenant with Noah, Abraham, Israel, David, and the promised "new covenant."

- New Testament writers use diathēkē when Jesus speaks of "the **new covenant** in my blood," and when Hebrews reflects on the "better covenant" He mediates.

Because diathēkē could also mean "will/testament," some passages (especially in Hebrews 9) play on that overlap:

- A covenant of promised benefits is like a **testament** that comes into force through **death**.

- Jesus' death is pictured as the moment when the **new covenant / new testament** is put into full effect.

This double sense is one reason our Bible is divided into **Old Testament** and **New Testament**—but the living idea behind both is still **covenant**.

3. Old and New: contrast, fulfillment, and continuity

When the New Testament speaks of a **"new covenant"**, it is drawing on prophetic promises (especially Jeremiah and Ezekiel).

The new covenant is:

- **New in quality** (often using the word kainos)—not just younger, but **fresh and transformed** in some way.

- **Linked** to the earlier covenants, not dropped from the sky. It fulfills Abraham's blessing, David's royal hope, and Torah's goal of a people who truly love God and neighbor.

- Marked by **forgiveness, internalized instruction** ("law written on hearts"), and the **gift of the Spirit**.

So how does it differ from what came before?

- The **Mosaic covenant** at Sinai was a national, law-centered administration. It was good, but fragile, because of human unfaithfulness.

- The **new covenant** centers on Jesus' self-giving and resurrection, and on the Spirit who transforms the heart.

- The same God, promises, and purposes run through both, but the **mode of relationship** is renewed and deepened.

This means:

- "Old covenant" vs "new covenant" is not simply "bad vs good" or "law vs grace," but **"earlier, preparatory form vs fulfilled, Spirit-filled form."**

- The New Testament does not cancel God's earlier covenants so much as **bring their true intention to maturity** in Christ.

4. Covenant vs rulebook, covenant vs mere "will"

Thinking in covenant terms corrects two common misunderstandings.

First, covenant is more than **law code**:

- Torah is the **instruction** of a covenant God, not just regulations.

- The covenant includes story, identity, worship, and promise, not only rules.

- Breaking covenant is primarily about **disloyalty** and **distrust**, not just technical infraction.

Second, covenant is more than a private **will**:

- A testament (in our sense) is usually a **one-sided document** about distributing possessions.

- A biblical covenant is **relational and communal**—a binding arrangement that shapes a people's entire way of life.

- When Hebrews uses the "will/testament" angle, it does so to highlight how **Jesus' death** enacts and guarantees the promised benefits of the covenant.

So:

- "Old Testament" and "New Testament" are best heard as "Old **Covenant** scriptures" and "New **Covenant** scriptures"—writings that witness to God's two major covenantal phases with His people.

- Both sections describe **one great story** of a God who binds Himself to humanity, calls a people, and keeps His promises at His own cost.

5. What did it say first—and how can we hear it now?

Listening back:

- **Berit** first said: **covenant**—a binding, often sacrificial, relational commitment in which God pledges Himself to a people and calls for loyal trust and obedience.

- **Diathēkē** carried that meaning into Greek, while also allowing a "**testament**" nuance that New Testament writers use to explain how Jesus' death brings the covenant blessings into force.

For us, that means:

- When you see "covenant," think **relationship with obligations**, not just "deal" or "contract."

- When you see "Old Testament" and "New Testament," remember you are holding the library of the **old-covenant era** and the **new--covenant era**, both telling the story of the same faithful God.

- When you hear "new covenant," think not only of something replacing what came before, but of God **renewing, deepening, and universalizing** His age-old promise: "I will be your God, and you will be My people."

Would it help if the next chapter ("Nations and Gentiles: Goyim and Ethnē") leans more into how covenant opens outward to all peoples, or stays tightly focused on the word study itself?

Chapter 29

Nations and Gentiles

Goyim and Ethnē

When English Bibles say **"nations"** or **"Gentiles,"** they often translate the same underlying words: **goyim** in Hebrew and **ethnē** in Greek. We may hear "other countries" or "non-Jews," but Scripture uses these words to talk about **peoples, identities, and God's global purpose**. The story moves from Israel **among** the nations to Israel as a blessing **for** the nations, until finally all nations are gathered in worship.

This chapter asks: What did **goy/goyim** and **ethnos/ethnē** say first? How did they come to mean "Gentiles"? And how do they connect to God's covenant promise to bless "all the families of the earth"?

1. Goy / Goyim: peoples, including Israel

In Hebrew, **goy** simply means a **people, nation, people-group**.

- It can refer to **any** nation: Egypt, Assyria, Babylon, or others around Israel.

- It can also refer to **Israel itself**: God calls Israel a **"goy qadosh"**—a **holy nation**.

So "goyim":

- Sometimes means **foreign nations**, especially those that do not know Israel's God.

- Sometimes carries a negative flavor when those nations are **idolatrous or hostile**.

- But at the basic level, it still means **peoples**, not "bad guys."

Key Old Testament themes:

- The nations are part of **God's creation and plan**; they are not an accident.

- Israel is chosen **from among the nations** to be a **light to the nations**.

- There is a tension: the nations **threaten** Israel's faithfulness, yet they are also the **intended recipients** of blessing.

From the start, God's covenant with Abraham includes the nations: "In you all the families of the earth shall be blessed." Israel's difference is ultimately for **the nations' good**.

2. Ethnos / Ethnē: nations, peoples, Gentiles

In Greek, **ethnos** (plural **ethnē**) also means:

- **Nation, people, ethnic group**, a collective defined by shared lineage, land, or culture.

In the Greek Old Testament:

- Ethnos translates **goy** and keeps its broad meaning: nations, peoples.

- Context decides whether it means Israel, other nations, or simply "peoples of the earth."

In the New Testament:

- Ethnē often means **"the nations"** in contrast to **Israel**.

- From that contrast comes the English habit of translating ethnē as **"Gentiles"**—non-Jewish peoples.

- Sometimes it must be read as **"nations"**, especially in global mission and worship passages ("all nations").

So:

- "Gentiles" is not a separate word so much as a **contextual meaning** of ethnē: the **non-Jewish nations**.

- If we always read "Gentiles," we may miss the **corporate, people-group** feel of the term.

3. From "the nations" vs Israel to "the nations" included

Throughout the Old Testament:

- **Israel vs the nations** is a central contrast: Israel is called to avoid the nations' idols and injustices.

- Yet Israel's **calling** is deeply **missionary**: to be a kingdom of priests, mediating God's blessing to the nations.

- Prophets foresee a day when the nations will **stream to Zion**, learning God's ways and sharing in His peace.

In the New Testament:

- Jesus' ministry begins within Israel, but His teaching and healings often hint at **inclusion of the nations** (Roman centurions, Samaritans, Canaanite women).

- After His death and resurrection, the commission is explicit: **"make disciples of all ethnē"**—all nations/peoples.

- The barrier between Israel and the nations is addressed in Christ: Gentiles are **grafted in, brought near, made fellow-citizens**.

This is not the erasure of Israel, but the **expansion of the covenant family**:

- The Abrahamic promise—blessing for all nations—comes into its **new-covenant phase**.

- Ethnē are no longer just "others out there"; they are welcomed **in** as co-heirs, while retaining their distinct peoples and cultures under Christ.

4. Nations, empire, and worship

Goyim/ethnē are not only targets of mission; they also represent **powers and systems**.

In Scripture:

- Empires like Egypt, Assyria, Babylon, and Rome are **nations** that can embody oppression and pride.

- God **judges** nations for violence, injustice, and idolatry, not just individuals.

- Yet even judged nations are also **invited** into repentance and future blessing.

In the end:

- Visions of the future show **all nations** bringing their glory into God's renewed city.

- People from **every tribe, tongue, and ethnos** worship the Lamb.

- "The nations" move from being often hostile to God's purposes to being **the multi-colored crowd of the redeemed**.

This means:

- Ethnē are not erased into a gray sameness; their **distinct identities** are preserved and offered in worship.

- God's covenant plan is **multi-ethnic by design**—the oneness He creates is not against diversity but **through** it.

5. What did it say first—and how can we hear it now?

Listening back:

- **Goy/goyim** first said: **nation(s), peoples**, including Israel itself—a neutral term that becomes positive or negative depending on the people's response to God.

- **Ethnos/ethnē** carried that forward as **nations/peoples**, which, in contrast to Israel, came to mean **non-Jews, the Gentiles**—but always as **corporate communities**, not just isolated individuals.

For us, that means:

- When you see "Gentiles," consider reading **"the nations"** or **"the other peoples"** in your mind, to recover the **people-group** sense.

- When you read about Israel and the nations, remember the **covenant arc**: chosen from the nations, for the nations, until all nations are invited into the covenant family in Christ.

- When you think about the church, picture a **multi-ethnic people** drawn from all ethnē, fulfilling the promise that in Abraham's seed **all the families of the earth** would be blessed.

Would you like the next chapter (30) to dig into how different canons highlight this nations-theme differently, or stay more on practical reading tools?

Part VI

Walking Forward With Better Ears

Books by Rene'

Reading With All the Canons in View

Most of us pick up a Bible and assume it is simply "the Bible." In reality, Christians have received **several closely related canons**—Jewish Tanakh, Protestant, Catholic, Orthodox, and Ethiopian lists that overlap heavily and differ at the edges. Those differences do not give us different Gods or different gospels, but they do shape which **words, names, and themes** we see, and how often we see them.

This chapter asks: What is a canon, how do the main Christian canons differ, and how can an ordinary reader **benefit** from all of them without feeling lost?

1. What a canon is (and isn't)

A **canon** is:

- The **recognized list of books** a community receives as Scripture.

- A **boundary line**: these books, not others, are read as uniquely authoritative in worship and doctrine.

A canon is **not**:

- A guarantee that every book is equally easy or equally central.

- A fence keeping you from ever reading anything outside it.

So when we talk about "canons," we are really talking about **which books are in the front row**, not which ideas are "in" or "out" of Christianity altogether.

2. The big picture: what all Christians share

Across all major Christian traditions:

- The **New Testament (27 books)** is the same.

- The central Old Testament story—**Torah, Prophets, and Writings**—is overwhelmingly shared.

- Core words and themes—creation, covenant, Torah, wisdom, sin, salvation, nations—are present everywhere.

If you read only a standard Protestant Bible, you still have:

- The full **Jesus story** and apostolic witness.

- The full **Torah and Prophets** that the New Testament constantly uses.

- The key vocabulary we have been exploring throughout this book.

This is why we can say: you can **fully hear the gospel** with any of the main canons.

3. Where the Old Testament canons differ

The differences show up in the **Old Testament**, especially in:

- Some wisdom and narrative books (e.g., Sirach, Wisdom of Solomon, Tobit, Judith).

- Additions to books you already know (e.g., extra sections in Daniel and Esther).

- A few other books in Orthodox and Ethiopian traditions.

These books:

- Often **fill in background**—expanding themes of wisdom, suffering, martyrdom, prayer, and hope.

- Are quoted or alluded to now and then in early Christian writings.

- Are treated as fully "Scripture" in Catholic and Orthodox churches, and as "useful but not canonical" in many Protestant contexts.

For our purposes:

- They add **extra windows** into words and ideas we already meet in the 66 books shared by all.

- They show how Jewish and early Christian communities were **already thinking** about things like covenant, law, nations, judgment, and resurrection.

4. Why canons matter for word and theme study

Canons shape which **examples** you see when you trace a word or theme.

For instance:

- **Wisdom and Torah**: books like Sirach and Wisdom of Solomon talk at length about **Torah as wisdom**, sharpening how we hear "law" as **life-giving instruction**, not just rules.

- **Nations and judgment**: some additional books have vivid prayers and stories about living among the nations, suffering under empire, and trusting God's justice.

- **Afterlife and resurrection**: later Jewish books sometimes develop ideas about resurrection and judgment in ways that echo into the New Testament.

If you only use one canon:

- You still have the **core data**.

- But you may miss some **in-between conversations** that help you see how certain words and themes were already being understood when the New Testament was written.

Using multiple canons:

- Doesn't change the **center** (Christ, the gospel, the shared Scriptures).

- Does enrich the **edges and background**, giving you more texture and context.

5. How to read with "all the canons" without getting overwhelmed

You don't need to become a canon expert to benefit. A few simple habits can help:

1. **Know what you have**

- Check which canon your main Bible follows (Protestant, Catholic, Orthodox).

- Notice which books are **extra** compared to the 39-book Protestant Old Testament.

1. **Keep the core and use the extras as windows**

- Treat the 66 books common to all as your **baseline**.

- Treat additional books as **side windows** that illuminate, not as new foundations.

1. **Follow themes across canons**

- When a topic matters—covenant, law, nations, wisdom, judgment—peek at how extra books talk about it.

- Ask: Does this **clarify how people in Jesus' day were already thinking**?

1. **Let differences make you curious, not anxious**

- If one tradition counts a book as Scripture and another as secondary, you can still **read it and learn**.

- Focus less on "Which shelf does this book sit on?" and more on "What does this book show about how God's people understood His words?"

6. What did it say first—and how can we hear it now?

Listening back:

- "Canon" first said: **a recognized list** of books a community trusts as Scripture.

- Different Christian canons highlight slightly different **collections**, while agreeing on the central story and vocabulary.

For us, that means:

- We can **trust our primary Bible** and still benefit from glancing over the fence at how other traditions receive and arrange the same story.

- When doing word and theme work, we can remember that the Bible we hold sits inside a **larger conversation**—Jewish, Catholic, Orthodox, Protestant—about God's words.

- Letting "all the canons" into view is less about adding rules and more about **hearing the same God** speak with a bit more historical and literary depth.

Would you like chapter 31 to stay tightly on practical tools (concordances, apps, notes), or to weave in one or two worked examples from earlier chapters as you go?

Chapter 31

Practical Tools for Ordinary Readers

You do not need to know Hebrew or Greek to benefit from what this book has been exploring. You do, however, need some **simple tools** and a few wise habits. This chapter is a short, practical guide to checking "what's under" your English Bible without getting lost in technical details.

1. Start with your main Bible and its notes

Your main Bible is still your **home base**.

- Use a **good translation** (or two): ideally one more "literal" (ESV, NASB, CSB, NRSV, etc.) and one more "dynamic" (NIV, NLT, etc.).

- Pay attention to **footnotes**: they often say "Or..." or "Hebrew/Greek...," hinting at where a word has a **wider range** than the English term shows.

- If your Bible has **cross-references**, use them: they link passages that use similar language or themes.

A simple habit: when a verse feels important or odd, glance down. Those tiny notes are often your first clue that there is more going on under the surface.

2. Use a basic concordance or search app

A **concordance** (or a Bible app with search) lets you:

- Look up every place a given **English word** appears ("law," "soul," "Gentiles," etc.).

- See **patterns**: where it clusters, how different authors use it, and how context shapes its sense.

Practical tips:

- On paper: use a concordance keyed to your translation; look up the English word, then skim the list of references.

- On a phone/computer: use a Bible app to search for the word and **scroll through** the hits.

- Always **read a few verses around** each hit so you don't rip the word out of context.

This doesn't tell you the underlying Hebrew/Greek yet, but it shows you how your **translation uses the English label**, which is often revealing in itself.

3. Check the underlying word with a simple lexicon tool

To see what's "underneath" an English term:

- Use a Bible app or website with **"interlinear"** or **"original language"** features.

- Tap or click the English word to see the **Hebrew/Greek term**, its basic glosses, and where else it appears.

Key cautions:

- Don't assume every occurrence of that Hebrew/Greek word has the **same meaning**; context still rules.

- Don't make too much of **roots** ("this word contains that word, so it must mean…"). Roots can help, but they can also mislead.

- Use lexicon entries (short dictionary definitions) as **guides**, not as magic keys.

Your goal is modest: to notice, "Ah, this 'law' is **Torah**," or "This 'Gentiles' is **ethnē**," and then remember what those words can mean.

4. Compare translations side-by-side

Different translations make **different choices** that can tip you off to a word's range.

Practical steps:

- Open two or three translations of the **same passage**.

- Note where they **diverge**: one says "justice," another "judgment"; one says "nations," another "Gentiles."

- Ask: "Why did they choose different words? What might the underlying term be able to mean?"

When several translations use **different English words**, that often means the original term has a **wide semantic range**. That's your cue to be curious, not suspicious.

5. Use word-study tools sparingly and wisely

There are many "word study" books and websites. Some are helpful; others overreach.

Wise use:

- Prefer tools that show you **real verse examples** rather than long speculative essays.

- Look for **modest claims**: "This word can mean A, B, or C, depending on context," not "This word secretly always means X in a mystical way."

- Use them to **confirm patterns** you already suspect from reading, not to replace reading.

A healthy pattern:

1. Notice something in your **Bible reading**.

2. Use **search and cross-references** to see it in a few other passages.

3. Check the **underlying word** and a brief lexicon entry.

4. Only then, if needed, glance at a more detailed **word-study resource**.

6. Ask good questions of every passage

No tool can replace good questions. For any verse or word:

- **Time and place**: When and where is this being written? What covenant setting?

- **Audience**: Israel in the land? Exiles? A small house church in a Roman city?

- **Word**: Which Hebrew/Greek term is under my English word? What else can it mean?

- **World**: What practices, institutions, or stories would that word evoke for them?

Even if you never look up a single Hebrew or Greek term, asking these questions will push you beyond "flat" readings and into **Bible-shaped sense**.

7. Keep it light, regular, and worshipful

The aim of these tools is not to make you a language scholar, but to help you:

- **Hear familiar verses freshly**.

- Avoid a few common mistakes (like assuming one English word maps to one precise ancient concept).

- Grow in **confidence and joy** as a reader.

A simple rhythm:

- Most days, just **read** and pray.

- Some days, when a word snags your attention, spend **five extra minutes** with a search, a second translation, or a quick word lookup.

- Now and then, pick one key term (like "covenant," "soul," or "nations") and trace it a bit further, using the tools from this chapter.

If you treat these tools as **servants to your listening**, not masters of your time, they will steadily deepen your sense that the Bible you already love is even **richer and more coherent** than you realized.

For chapter 32, would you prefer a big-picture walk through the Bible's story using the words we've studied, or a set of shorter vignettes showing how these word insights change specific passages?

Hearing the Bible's Big Story in Its Own Words

This book has walked through names, words, and canons—YHWH and "LORD," nephesh and "soul," Torah and "law," berit and "covenant," goyim and "Gentiles," Sheol and "hell." The goal was never vocabulary for its own sake. It was to help you hear the **one great story** of Scripture in the tones and textures its first hearers knew. This final chapter sketches that story using the words we've met, then shows briefly how listening for them can change the way familiar passages sound.

1. Creation, image, and calling

The story begins with **Elohim**, the one God, creating the heavens and the earth and forming **adam**—humanity—in His **image**.

- Humans are made to reflect God's **character and rule** into the world, not as gods but as **image-bearers**.

- Each person is a **nephesh**—a living, breathing being—not a ghost in a machine but an integrated whole of body, breath, and life.

- God's world is marked by **shalom**—wholeness, harmony, right relationship.

From the start, humanity's calling is covenant-shaped: to live as **partners** in

God's wise rule, tending creation and one another in trust and obedience.

2. Sin, fracture, and the first promises

Very quickly, humans **miss the mark**—they **chata'** and **hamartia**—turning from trust to self-rule.

- Sin is not just rule-breaking; it is **misdirected love**, a refusal to trust the Creator.

- The result is **death** in layers: spiritual estrangement, relational rupture, and physical mortality.

- The ground is cursed, labor becomes toil, and the image is **marred but not erased**.

Yet from within the curse, God speaks **promise**—offspring who will crush the serpent, hints that sin and death will not have the last word. Even here, **mishpat** (judgment) and **mercy** are bound together: God confronts evil yet clothes the guilty and keeps the story going.

3. Covenant: berit with a people for the nations

Rather than abandoning creation, God tightens the lens.

- With **Noah**, God makes a **berit** never again to destroy all flesh with a flood.

- With **Abraham**, God binds Himself to a family: "I will bless you… and in you all the **goyim**, all the families of the earth, will be blessed."

- With **Israel at Sinai**, God makes a **covenant**: "I will be your God, and you will be My people," giving **Torah** as His **instruction** for a liberated people.

Torah is not a cold law code; it is **teaching** framed by the story of rescue—"I brought you out of Egypt, therefore live this way." Israel is to be a **holy goy**, a set-apart nation, a **qahal** (assembly) of God, living out His **tsedaqah** (righteousness/justice) and **mishpat** as a light among the **ethnē**.

4. Failure, exile, and deepened hope

Israel's story is shot through with failure.

- Kings and people alike fall into **avon** and **anomia**—crookedness and lawlessness.

- Prophets announce God's **krisis**—His judgment—through drought, defeat, and eventually **exile**.

- The land is lost, the temple destroyed, and God's people are scattered among the nations.

Yet the prophets also speak **new words of hope**:

- A **new covenant** (berit chadashah) where Torah is written on hearts, not just stone.

- A **Servant** who bears iniquity.

- A **Son of David**, a **Son of Man**, a Spirit-anointed ruler who will bring true **shalom**.

- The **nations** streaming to Zion, swords beaten into plowshares.

The story's tension sharpens: How can a holy God **forgive** and **restore** without ignoring justice? How will His **name** be honored among the nations if His own people are faithless?

5. Jesus: Yeshua, Messiah, Son of God, Son of Man

Into this tension steps **Yeshua**—Jesus, whose name means "YHWH saves."

- He is proclaimed as **Messiah/Christos**—God's anointed king from David's line.

- He is called **Son of God**—Israel's calling, the king's title, and more, all converging.

- He names Himself **Son of Man**—the Human One, resonating with Daniel's vision of a figure who receives an everlasting kingdom.

Jesus **embodies** Torah: He fulfills its **aim** of love for God and neighbor, and exposes interpretations that turned it into a heavy rulebook. He brings **mishpat** and **tsedaqah** together—calling out hypocrisy, lifting the poor, forgiving sinners, and announcing **good news** of the **kingdom of God**.

He also speaks with terrifying clarity:

- Warns of **Gehenna**, outer darkness, and **weeping and gnashing of teeth** as images of what it means to reject God's kingdom.

- Tells of a coming **krisis**, a day when everything hidden will be revealed.

- Yet continually offers **metanoia**—repentance, a change of mind and direction.

In His life, the story's key words take on flesh.

6. Cross, resurrection, Spirit: the new covenant in His blood

At the cross, Jesus gathers the story's threads into a single, costly act.

- He shares a final meal, speaking of **"the new diathēkē in my blood"**—the new covenant/"testament" sealed by His death.

- On the cross, sin is **judged** and **borne**; God's **mishpat** against evil and His **charis** (grace) toward sinners meet.

- His body is laid among the dead—He truly enters **Hades**, the realm of the dead.

On the third day, He is raised:

- His resurrection is the **firstfruits** of a new creation, the pledge that **death and Hades** will not rule forever.

- Later visions show **death and Hades** thrown into the **lake of fire**, the **second death**, so that death itself is judged and undone.

At Pentecost, He pours out the **pneuma**—the Spirit.

- The Spirit writes **Torah on hearts**, fulfilling new-covenant promises.

- A new **ekklesia** (church) forms—God's **qahal** reborn—spanning Judea, Samaria, and the **ethnē**.

- This community is called to live as a **multi-ethnic image-bearing people**, anticipating the renewal of all things.

7. From Israel and the nations to every tribe and tongue

The gospel spreads.

- Paul speaks of **dikaiosynē** (righteousness) by **pistis** (faith/faithfulness), open to **Jew and Greek** alike.

- The barrier between **Israel and the nations** is dismantled in Christ; **ethnē** are no longer outsiders but fellow heirs.

- The church is called to embody God's **justice and mercy**, to live as a **holy ethnos**, a people of every language and culture.

Yet tension remains:

- Believers still struggle with **sarx** (flesh), with sin and suffering.

- The world still knows war, injustice, and death.

- The New Testament speaks of a coming **aiōn**—age—when God's kingdom will be fully manifest.

The story now moves on two tracks: **already** (Christ is risen, the Spirit has been given) and **not yet** (creation still groans, awaiting full **apokatastasis**—restoration).

8. Judgment, hell, and the end of evil

Scripture's final visions use the strongest images we have traced:

- A **great white throne** and a **krisis** according to deeds.

- A **lake of fire**, the **second death**, where death, Hades, and all unrepentant evil meet their end.

- Images of **Gehenna**, of **outer darkness**, of those who persist in rejecting God's life.

Christians have differed on the **how**—eternal conscious separation, final destruction, or ultimately healing judgment—but Scripture is united on the **that**:

- Evil will be **fully exposed and decisively dealt with**.

- God's **tsedaqah and mishpat** will be seen as good and true.

- There is a real tragedy in refusing God's offered life.

God's judgments are not arbitrary; they are the **final outworking** of all the words we've studied: covenant faithfulness, patient mercy, and holy opposition to all that destroys His beloved creation.

9. New creation: shalom, presence, and praise

The story ends where it began—but deeper and richer.

- A **new heavens and new earth**: creation renewed, not discarded.

- God dwelling with His people; no more **death, mourning, crying, or pain**.

- The **nations** bringing their glory into the city; every **ethnos** represented around the throne.

Here, key words find their final home:

- **Shalom** is complete—everything in its right place, in right relationship.

- **Berit** is fulfilled—God's covenant promise kept beyond all expectation.

- **Torah** is fully internalized—God's instruction is no longer resisted but delighted in.

- **Image** is restored—humans reigning with God, reflecting His character without distortion.

God's name—**YHWH**, revealed in Jesus—is honored. The whole creation becomes a temple, and every nephesh lives in the light of God.

10. Walking forward with better ears

You now have a set of ears tuned, however lightly, to the **tones under the English words**.

As you keep reading:

- Let "LORD" remind you of **YHWH**, the personal, covenant name of the God who acts.

- Let "law" remind you of **Torah**, God's instructing of a people He has already rescued.

- Let "soul," "spirit," "flesh," and "body" remind you of **whole, embodied persons** and of the Spirit's renewing work.

- Let "covenant" and "testament" remind you of **berit and diathēkē**, of a God who binds Himself to His people.

- Let "nations" and "Gentiles" remind you that the story is **world-wide**, not just personal.

- Let "hell," "judgment," and "heaven" remind you of all the images—Sheol, Hades, Gehenna, lake of fire, new creation—that together insist God will **judge evil and heal creation**.

You do not need to memorize the foreign terms. You only need to remember that behind your English Bible is a **coherent, story-shaped world of words,** all centered on the God revealed in Jesus. As you listen for those echoes, you will find that familiar verses open up—not to make you clever, but to draw you more deeply into **trust, worship, and faithful living** in the story they tell.

Part VII

Appendices

A. GLOSSARY OF KEY TERMS

Adam – Hebrew word meaning "human" or "humanity"; also the name of the first human in Genesis.

Adonai – Hebrew title meaning "Lord" or "Master," used for God as ruler and covenant king.

Aiōn – Greek word for "age" or "era"; can mean a long period of time or the world-order of a given age.

Aiōnios – Greek adjective from aiōn; "of the age," often translated "eternal" or "everlasting."

Anthrōpos – Greek word for "human being" or "person," used for individuals and humanity in general.

Apokatastasis – Greek term meaning "restoration"; used for the idea of restoring things to their proper state.

Avon – Hebrew word for "iniquity" or "crookedness"; guilt and twisted wrongdoing and its consequences.

Basar – Hebrew word for "flesh"; can mean body, physical life, or kin (family).

Berit – Hebrew word for "covenant"; a binding, relational agreement with promises and obligations.

Charis – Greek word for "grace," "favor," or "gift"; God's free, generous kindness toward us.

Chata' – Hebrew verb for "to miss the mark," often translated "to sin."

Christ / Christos – Greek for "Anointed One"; the title "Christ" is equivalent to "Messiah," God's chosen king.

Covenant – A solemn, relational agreement between parties, often with promises, signs, and responsibilities.

Diathēkē – Greek word usually meaning "covenant," sometimes "testament" or "will."

Dikaiosynē – Greek word for "righteousness"; being in the right, living in line with God's will.

Eirēnē – Greek word for "peace"; not just lack of conflict, but wholeness and harmony, like shalom.

Ekklesia – Greek word for "assembly" or "gathering"; used for the church as God's gathered people.

Elohim – Hebrew word for "God"; grammatically plural but usually refers to Israel's one God.

Ethnos / Ethnē – Greek for "nation" or "people-group"; in many contexts, "the nations" or "the Gentiles."

Gehenna – Greek form of "Valley of Hinnom," a real valley near Jerusalem; used as an image of final judgment.

Goy / Goyim – Hebrew word for "nation" / "nations"; can refer to any people, including Israel, or to other nations.

Hamartia – Greek word for "sin"; literally "missing the mark," choosing wrongly against God.

Hades – Greek term for the realm of the dead; used in the New Testament for the place of the dead before final judgment.

Heart / Lev – Hebrew "lev" means the inner person: mind, will, and emotions, not just feelings.

Hesed – Hebrew word for loyal love, covenant faithfulness, and kindness.

Image of God – The status and calling of humans to reflect God's character and rule into creation.

Judgment / Krisis – Greek "krisis" means decision, judgment, or separation; God's truthful verdict and setting things right.

Kardia – Greek word for "heart"; the inner self, including thoughts, desires, and will.

Koinōnia – Greek word for "fellowship" or "sharing"; close participation in life together.

Kyrios – Greek word for "Lord"; used in the Greek Old Testament for God and in the New Testament for Jesus.

Lake of fire – Revelation's image for the final, decisive judgment of evil, called "the second death."

Law / Nomos – Greek "nomos" translates "Torah"; can mean law, instruction, or the covenant way of life.

Logos – Greek for "word," "reason," or "message"; in John 1, a title for Jesus as God's self-expression.

Mishpat – Hebrew word for "judgment" or "justice"; God's decisions and the just order that results.

Mo'ed – Hebrew word for "appointed time" or "appointed festival."

Nephesh – Hebrew word for "living being," "life," or "self"; often translated "soul," but means the whole living person.

Pneuma – Greek word for "spirit," "breath," or "wind"; used for human spirit and the Holy Spirit.

Pistis – Greek for "faith," "trust," and "faithfulness"; reliance on God and loyalty to Him.

Qahal – Hebrew word for "assembly" or "gathering," especially of God's people.

Ruach – Hebrew for "wind," "breath," or "spirit"; used of God's Spirit and human spirit.

Salvation / Yasha' – Hebrew root for "to save," "to deliver," "to make wide or safe"; God's rescue and help.

Sarx – Greek for "flesh"; human weakness and mortality, and sometimes the sphere of life opposed to God.

Second death – Revelation's term for the final, ultimate death linked with the lake of fire.

Sheol – Hebrew term for the realm of the dead; a shadowy underworld where the dead go.

Shalom – Hebrew word for "peace" as wholeness, completeness, well-being, and right relationship.

Sin – Any thought, action, or state that turns away from God's will and distorts love.

Soul – English word often used for nephesh or psychē; in Scripture usually refers to the whole living person, not just a ghost-like part.

Spirit – English word for ruach/pneuma; God's active presence or the inner life of a person.

Testament – English term for "covenant" or "will"; used in "Old Testament" and "New Testament" for the two main parts of the Christian Bible.

Torah – Hebrew word for "instruction" or "teaching"; often used for the first five books of the Bible and for God's covenant guidance to Israel.

Tsedaqah – Hebrew word for "righteousness" or "justice"; living in right relationship with God and others.

Word of God – God's speech, message, or self-revelation; in the New Testament, also a title for Jesus (the Logos).

YHWH – The personal name of God in the Hebrew Bible, often rendered "LORD" in English Bibles.

Yeshua / Jesus – Hebrew/Aramaic and Greek forms of the name meaning "YHWH saves."

Yasha' – Hebrew root behind "salvation"; to rescue, deliver, and bring into safety and spaciousness.

Zion – The hill in Jerusalem associated with the temple; often a symbol for God's dwelling and His people.

B. WORD INDEX

(ENGLISH   HEBREW/GREEK)

Word Index: English Terms and Main Hebrew/Greek Equivalents

Adam – Hebrew: adam; Greek: anthrōpos

Age – Hebrew: olam; Greek: aiōn

Angels – Hebrew: mal'akhim; Greek: angeloi

Assembly – Hebrew: qahal; Greek: ekklēsia

Body – Hebrew: basar; Greek: sōma

Breath – Hebrew: ruach, neshamah; Greek: pneuma

Covenant – Hebrew: berit; Greek: diathēkē

Creation – Hebrew: bara'; Greek: ktisis

Darkness (spiritual) – Hebrew: choshekh; Greek: skotos

Death – Hebrew: mavet; Greek: thanatos

Deliver / Save – Hebrew: yasha'; Greek: sōzō

Devil / Adversary – Hebrew: satan; Greek: diabolos, satanas

Earth / Land – Hebrew: erets; Greek: gē

Eternal / Everlasting – Hebrew: olam; Greek: aiōnios

Exile – Hebrew: galut, gola; Greek: metoikesia

Faith / Faithfulness – Hebrew: 'emunah, aman; Greek: pistis

Flesh – Hebrew: basar; Greek: sarx

Forgive / Forgiveness – Hebrew: salah; Greek: aphesis, aphiemi

Gentiles – Hebrew: goyim; Greek: ethnē

Glory – Hebrew: kavod; Greek: doxa

God – Hebrew: Elohim, El; Greek: Theos

Grace / Favor – Hebrew: ḥen; Greek: charis

Grave – Hebrew: qeber; Greek: mnēmeion

Heart – Hebrew: lev; Greek: kardia

Hell (realm of dead / judgment) – Hebrew: Sheol; Greek: Hades, Gehenna, Tartarus

Holy / Holiness – Hebrew: qadosh; Greek: hagios, hagiasmos

Image (of God) – Hebrew: tselem, demut; Greek: eikōn, homoiōsis

Iniquity – Hebrew: avon; Greek: adikia, anomia

Judge (verb) – Hebrew: shafat; Greek: krinō

Judgment – Hebrew: mishpat; Greek: krisis

King – Hebrew: melek; Greek: basileus

Kingdom – Hebrew: malkut; Greek: basileia

Knowledge – Hebrew: da'at; Greek: gnōsis, epignōsis

Law – Hebrew: Torah; Greek: nomos

Life – Hebrew: chayyim; Greek: zōē, bios

Light – Hebrew: 'or; Greek: phōs

Lord (title) – Hebrew: Adonai; Greek: kyrios

LORD (name of God) – Hebrew: YHWH; Greek: kyrios (in LXX)

Love – Hebrew: 'ahavah, hesed; Greek: agapē, philia

Mercy – Hebrew: rachamim, hesed; Greek: eleos

Messiah / Christ – Hebrew: mashiach; Greek: Christos

Name – Hebrew: shem; Greek: onoma

Nation(s) – Hebrew: goy, goyim; Greek: ethnos, ethnē

Peace – Hebrew: shalom; Greek: eirēnē

People (of God) – Hebrew: 'am; Greek: laos

Praise – Hebrew: halal, tehillah; Greek: aineō, doxazō

Prophet – Hebrew: navi'; Greek: prophētēs

Repent / Repentance – Hebrew: shuv; Greek: metanoeō, metanoia

Rescue – Hebrew: yasha', natzal; Greek: sōzō, rhyomai

Resurrection – Hebrew: (concept) t'chiyyat hametim; Greek: anastasis

Rest / Sabbath – Hebrew: shabbat, nuach; Greek: sabbaton, anapausis

Righteous / Righteousness – Hebrew: tsaddiq, tsedaqah; Greek: dikaios, dikaiosynē

Sacrifice – Hebrew: zevach, korban; Greek: thusia

Salvation – Hebrew: yeshu'ah; Greek: sōtēria

Sanctify / Make Holy – Hebrew: qadash; Greek: hagiazō

Satan / Adversary – Hebrew: satan; Greek: satanas

Sheol (underworld) – Hebrew: Sheol; Greek: Hades (often), sometimes translated indirectly

Sin – Hebrew: chata', pesha', avon; Greek: hamartia, anomia

Soul – Hebrew: nephesh; Greek: psychē

Spirit – Hebrew: ruach; Greek: pneuma

Temple – Hebrew: heikal, beit-haMikdash; Greek: hieron, naos

Testament – (see Covenant) Hebrew: berit; Greek: diathēkē

Throne – Hebrew: kise'; Greek: thronos

Time (appointed) – Hebrew: mo'ed; Greek: kairos

Transgression – Hebrew: pesha'; Greek: parabasis

Truth – Hebrew: 'emet; Greek: alētheia

Wisdom – Hebrew: chokmah; Greek: sophia

Word – Hebrew: davar; Greek: logos, rhēma

World – Hebrew: erets, tevel; Greek: kosmos

Wrath – Hebrew: 'af, chemah; Greek: orgē

YHWH (the Name) – Hebrew: YHWH; Greek: kyrios (in LXX), rendered "LORD" in English

C. SCRIPTURE INDEX

(ALL CANONS CLEARLY MARKED)

J – Jewish Tanakh

P – Protestant

C – Roman Catholic

O – Eastern / Oriental Orthodox (Septuagint-based)

E – Ethiopian Orthodox Tewahedo (core 81-book canon)

I list each book once, with its marker string (e.g., **P/C/O/E**).

Torah / Pentateuch

Genesis – J/P/C/O/E

Exodus – J/P/C/O/E

Leviticus – J/P/C/O/E

Numbers – J/P/C/O/E

Deuteronomy – J/P/C/O/E

Historical Books (Shared Core)

Joshua – J/P/C/O/E

Judges – J/P/C/O/E

Ruth – J/P/C/O/E

1 Samuel – J/P/C/O/E

2 Samuel – J/P/C/O/E

1 Kings – J/P/C/O/E

2 Kings – J/P/C/O/E

1 Chronicles – J/P/C/O/E

2 Chronicles – J/P/C/O/E

Ezra – J/P/C/O/E

Nehemiah – J/P/C/O/E

Esther (Hebrew form) – J/P/C/O

Historical Books (Deuterocanonical / Apocryphal)

Tobit – C/O/E

Judith – C/O/E

Greek Esther (additions) – C/O/E

1 Maccabees – C/O

2 Maccabees – C/O

3 Maccabees – O (some traditions)

4 Maccabees – O (appendix in some editions)

1 Esdras – O (and some C as deuterocanonical)

2 Esdras (sometimes called 4 Ezra) – O (varied); in some Latin appendices

Prayer of Manasseh – O (often included; sometimes in C appendices)

Poetry and Wisdom (Shared Core)

Job – J/P/C/O/E

Psalms – J/P/C/O/E

Proverbs – J/P/C/O/E

Ecclesiastes (Qoheleth) – J/P/C/O/E

Song of Songs (Song of Solomon) – J/P/C/O/E

Poetry and Wisdom (Deuterocanonical / Apocryphal)

Wisdom of Solomon – C/O/E

Sirach (Ecclesiasticus) – C/O/E

Psalm 151 – O/E (not in P/C)

Major Prophets (Shared Core)

Isaiah – J/P/C/O/E

Jeremiah – J/P/C/O/E

Lamentations – J/P/C/O/E

Ezekiel – J/P/C/O/E

Daniel (Hebrew form) – J/P/C/O/E

Prophetic / Deuterocanonical Additions

Baruch (including Letter of Jeremiah) – C/O

Letter of Jeremiah (counted with Baruch in C; separate in some O) – C/O

Greek additions to Daniel

Susanna – C/O

Bel and the Dragon – C/O

Prayer of Azariah and Song of the Three – C/O

The Twelve Minor Prophets (Shared Core)

(All twelve are J/P/C/O/E)

Hosea – J/P/C/O/E

Joel – J/P/C/O/E

Amos – J/P/C/O/E

Obadiah – J/P/C/O/E

Jonah – J/P/C/O/E

Micah – J/P/C/O/E

Nahum – J/P/C/O/E

Habakkuk – J/P/C/O/E

Zephaniah – J/P/C/O/E

Haggai – J/P/C/O/E

Zechariah – J/P/C/O/E

Malachi – J/P/C/O/E

Additional Old Testament Books in Ethiopian Canon

(These are part of E; not in P/C/O/J canons)

1 Enoch – E

Jubilees – E

1 Meqabyan – E

2 Meqabyan – E

3 Meqabyan – E

(Various church-order and covenant books appear in the broader E canon, but those go beyond the main 81-book list.)

New Testament (Same 27 in P/C/O/J-Christian; E includes these plus extra church-order works)

Gospels

Matthew – P/C/O/E

Mark – P/C/O/E

Luke – P/C/O/E

John – P/C/O/E

History

Acts – P/C/O/E

Pauline Letters

Romans – P/C/O/E

1 Corinthians – P/C/O/E

2 Corinthians – P/C/O/E

Galatians – P/C/O/E

Ephesians – P/C/O/E

Philippians – P/C/O/E

Colossians – P/C/O/E

1 Thessalonians – P/C/O/E

2 Thessalonians – P/C/O/E

1 Timothy – P/C/O/E

2 Timothy – P/C/O/E

Titus – P/C/O/E

Philemon – P/C/O/E

Hebrews – P/C/O/E

Catholic (General) Letters

James – P/C/O/E

1 Peter – P/C/O/E

2 Peter – P/C/O/E

1 John – P/C/O/E

2 John – P/C/O/E

3 John – P/C/O/E

Jude – P/C/O/E

Apocalypse

Revelation – P/C/O/E

Additional New Testament-Related Works in Ethiopian Canon (Broader Church-Order Section)

(Counted in the broader Ethiopian New Testament collection)

Sinodos (4 books of church canons) – E

1 Covenant – E

2 Covenant – E

Ethiopic Clement – E

Ethiopic Didascalia – E

D. VISUAL TIMELINE OF CANONS AND KEY DEVELOPMENTS

"Different Christian traditions arrange the same core story with a few extra windows. This timeline shows how those canons emerged over time. "This book is meant to be read with your Bible open and your curiosity awake. You do not need to know any Hebrew or Greek; you only need a willingness to slow down and ask, "What did this word say first?"

Timeline: From Scrolls to Canons

c. 1400–400 BCE – Writing of the Old Testament books

Torah (Genesis–Deuteronomy), then Prophets and Writings, are composed over many centuries.

Israel copies and reads individual scrolls; there is no single "book" yet.

c. 300–100 BCE – Greek translation: the Septuagint (LXX)

Hebrew Scriptures begin to be translated into Greek for Jews in the Greek-speaking world.

The Septuagint includes the familiar books plus several others (Tobit, Sirach, Wisdom, Maccabees, additions to Daniel/Esther, etc.).

This Greek collection becomes the "Bible" for many early Jews and most early Christians.

1st century CE – New Testament writings

Gospels, letters, and Revelation are written and circulated among churches.

Christians use the Jewish Scriptures (mostly in Greek) alongside these new writings.

There is functional authority before there is a closed list.

2nd–3rd centuries CE – Emerging Christian Old and New Testaments

Core New Testament books are widely recognized (Gospels, Paul's letters, Acts).

The Septuagint remains the main Old Testament for most churches.

Some books are disputed or used regionally (Hebrews, Revelation, a few others).

4th century CE – Formal recognition of the 27-book New Testament

Church leaders and councils recognize the 27 books we know today as the New Testament.

There is strong convergence across East and West on this list.

Old Testament usage continues to follow the Septuagint in most churches.

Rabbinic Judaism – Tanakh structure clarified

Jewish communities clarify and teach the three-part structure: **Torah, Prophets, Writings.**

The core 24-book Hebrew canon (equivalent to 39 Protestant OT books) is in place.

Books found only in Greek are generally not treated as Scripture in the same way.

Medieval period – Western (Latin) church and the Vulgate

Latin translations (especially the Vulgate) become standard in the West.

The Latin Old Testament includes the deuterocanonical books used in the Septuagint tradition.

East (Greek) and West (Latin) both use a **larger Old Testament** than the later Protestant canon.

16th century – Reformation and Protestant canon

Protestant Reformers affirm the 27-book New Testament with the historic church.

For the Old Testament, they follow the **Hebrew canon**, placing the extra Greek books in a separate "Apocrypha" section or omitting them from the main list.

Catholic and Orthodox traditions continue to treat many of these as Scripture (now called **deuterocanonical** in Catholic use).

Catholic Church – Deuterocanonical books reaffirmed

The Catholic Church reaffirms the Old Testament including Tobit, Judith, Wisdom, Sirach, Baruch, 1–2 Maccabees, and additions to Esther and Daniel as canonical.

These, with the 27 New Testament books, make up the Catholic Bible.

Orthodox Churches – Septuagint-based Old Testament

Orthodox traditions keep a **Septuagint-shaped Old Testament**, often including additional books such as 3 Maccabees, Psalm 151, and 1 Esdras.

Lists vary slightly by jurisdiction but share a common Septuagint heritage.

Ethiopian Orthodox Tewahedo Church – Wider canon

The Ethiopian Church recognizes a broader Old Testament that includes books like 1 Enoch, Jubilees, and the three Meqabyan books.

Its New Testament includes the standard 27 plus additional church-order writings (Sinodos, Covenant books, Ethiopic Clement, etc.).

Modern era – Printed and digital Bibles

Most printed Protestant Bibles contain 66 books (39 OT + 27 NT).

Catholic Bibles contain 73 books; Orthodox and Ethiopian Bibles contain more, depending on tradition.

Study Bibles, apps, and parallel editions now make it easier to **see multiple canon traditions side by side**.

Afterword

WHEN IT FEELS LIKE TOO MUCH

You have just walked through canons, word ranges, Hebrew and Greek terms, and some of Scripture's deepest themes. It is normal, at this point, to feel both **excited and overwhelmed**. This final word is here to say: that is okay—and to remind you what all of this is for.

1. You are not late to the party

Christians have been reading the Bible for two thousand years.

- You are not expected to catch up to the whole history of interpretation.

- You are invited to join the conversation **right where you are**, with what you now know.

- Every new insight belongs in a life-long process, not in an exam you have to pass.

If you feel behind, remember: the point is not to become a walking word-study, but to become a person who **hears God's voice more clearly**.

2. Let love set the pace

Knowledge can puff up or build up.

Ask of every new detail:

- "How does this help me **love God** with heart, soul, mind, and strength?"

- "How does this move me toward **loving my neighbor** more wisely and concretely?"

If a word study makes you more patient with others, more honest with yourself, or more drawn to prayer and obedience, it is doing exactly what it should. If it only makes you want to win arguments, slow down and ask God to **re-aim your curiosity**.

3. Stay anchored in simple reading and prayer

All the tools in the world are supplements to the basics:

- **Read**: keep a steady habit of reading whole chapters and books, not just verses.

- **Pray**: ask God to use His words to search, comfort, and guide you.

- **Belong**: talk about what you read with other believers; listen to how others hear the same texts.

You might choose:

- One or two days a week where you **don't look anything up**—you simply read and respond.

- One day where you give yourself an extra ten minutes with a concordance or app.

Let the **relationship** stay central and the research stay supportive.

4. Trust your English Bible—and look under the surface when needed

This whole book has been about what lies **under** our English translations.

That does not mean your Bible is untrustworthy.

You can:

- Read with confidence that the **main story and message** are clear in your language.

- Use word insights to **clarify**, not to constantly doubt every verse.

- Treat "What's the word under this?" as a **bonus question**, not a requirement.

Most of the time, the translation you have is more than enough to lead you to Christ, shape your life, and sustain your hope.

5. Welcome limits and keep going

You will forget terms. You will misapply an insight. You will discover, later, that something you thought was simple is more complex.

That's normal.

- God does not ask you to master His Word as an object.

- He invites you to **live in it**, like a home where you gradually notice more details.

- Over time, as you revisit passages, the words you've learned—Torah, berit, shalom, nephesh, mishpat, ethnē—will quietly deepen what you hear.

When it feels like too much, come back to something simple and solid:

- A psalm prayed slowly.

- A gospel story read with attention.

- A promise about God's faithful love.

Let those anchor you while the rest settles in its own time.

6. The point of better ears

At every stage, the goal is the same:

- To see God as Scripture shows Him: holy and merciful, just and patient.

- To see yourself truthfully: created in His image, broken by sin, loved and called in Christ.

- To see others as Scripture does: neighbors, enemies, brothers and sisters, all of them people for whom Christ died.

If these pages have given you even a slightly clearer hearing of that story, they have done their job. The rest is a life-long invitation:

Keep reading. Keep asking. Keep listening. And let the God whose words you study be the One you **trust, worship, and follow**.

Epilogue

An epilogue is where a book turns around and looks back at the path it has walked. This one began with a simple question: **what did it say first?** We have followed that question through names, titles, and everyday words—through "LORD" and "Jesus," "Son of God" and "Son of Man," "soul" and "spirit," "flesh," "heart," "grave," and "love." At each step, we have tried to listen to Scripture on its own terms before we rushed to our own.

Along the way, three themes have surfaced again and again.

First, **the Bible's words are richer than our shortcuts.** Behind "LORD" stands YHWH, the One who told Moses, "I will be who I will be," and promised to be with His people. Behind "Jesus" stands Yeshua—"YHWH saves"—and the long story of Joshua and God's saving acts. Behind "Christ" stand oil, kings, priests, and the hope of a coming anointed ruler. Behind "Son of God" and "Son of Man" stand Israel, David, Ezekiel, Daniel, and Second Temple hopes. Scripture's vocabulary is not a set of bare labels; it is **thick with story.**

Second, **the Bible's view of the human person is more integrated than ours.** We often divide ourselves into body and soul, head and heart, spiritual and physical. The Bible speaks of **nephesh** and **ruach**, of **heart** and **flesh**, of **body** and **spirit** in ways that resist easy diagrams. You are not a ghost in a machine. You are a living soul, an embodied self, dust and breath together, whose heart—mind, will, desires, and emotions—stands open before God. When Scripture speaks of saving souls, renewing hearts, raising bodies, or pouring out the Spirit, it speaks to **the whole person**.

Third, judgment and hope are more textured than a single word like "hell" suggests. We have seen that Sheol and Hades speak of the realm of the dead; that Gehenna grows from a real valley of idolatry and fire into an image of God's final judgment; that Tartarus names a deep prison for rebellious angels. Scripture holds together both the seriousness of judgment and the possibility of rescue from the grave. It refuses to flatten death and beyond into one neat diagram. Instead, it keeps us listening to promises: that God will not abandon His holy one to Sheol, that death will be swallowed up, that there will be a resurrection of the just and the unjust, that God will make all things new.

None of this is meant to turn you into a specialist in Hebrew and Greek. It is meant to give you **better ears**. When you see small caps LORD, you can remember a name and a promise. When you read "Jesus," you can hear "YHWH saves." When you hear "Christ," you can remember anointed king, priest, and prophet. When you see "heart," you can think "my whole inner self," not only my feelings. When you see "soul," you can think "my life, my self before God," not a ghost that might someday escape my body. When you see "hell," you can pause and ask which word stands behind it, and what picture it first painted.

This book has not tried to answer every question or solve every debate. It has simply tried to **slow you down**, to put some of our most familiar words back into their original homes so their color and weight can return. If that has happened even a little—if you now stumble for half a second over "LORD" or "Christ" or "soul" and think, "Wait, what did this say first?"—then the journey has been worthwhile.

The final goal, however, is not better word studies. It is **clearer worship and truer obedience**. To know that the God you call "Lord" is the One who brought Israel out of Egypt and raised Jesus from the dead; to know that the Savior you call "Jesus" carries the name "YHWH saves"; to know that the Spirit who lives in you is the same breath that hovered over the waters and raised Christ; to know that your heart, your soul, your body, your whole self are seen and claimed by this God—these are not mere details. They are reasons to trust Him more deeply, to love Him more fully, and to follow Him more faithfully in the ordinary words and days of your life.

If you come away from this book with one habit, let it be this: **whenever a familiar Bible word appears, ask what it said first, and then let that answer widen what it says to you now.** Over time, that simple practice can turn thin, churchy language back into the living, surprising, demanding, hopeful speech it was when God first spoke and people first listened.

-
-
-
-
-
-
-
-
-
-

-
-
-
-
-
-
-
-
-
-
-
-
-
-
-

-
-
-
-
-
-
-
-
-
-
-
-
-
-
-

-
-
-
-

Bibliography

General Introductions to Scripture and Theology

Bartholomew, Craig G., and Michael W. Goheen. *The Drama of Scripture: Finding Our Place in the Biblical Story*. 2nd ed. Grand Rapids: Baker Academic, 2014.

Bird, Michael F. *Seven Things I Wish Christians Knew about the Bible*. Grand Rapids: Zondervan, 2021.

Childs, Brevard S. *Introduction to the Old Testament as Scripture*. Philadelphia: Fortress Press, 1979.

Enns, Peter. *Inspiration and Incarnation: Evangelicals and the Problem of the Old Testament*. 2nd ed. Grand Rapids: Baker Academic, 2015.

Goldingay, John. *Do We Need the New Testament? Letting the Old Testament Speak for Itself*. Downers Grove, IL: IVP Academic, 2015.

Goldsworthy, Graeme. *According to Plan: The Unfolding Revelation of God in the Bible*. Downers Grove, IL: IVP, 1991.

Longman, Tremper III. *How to Read the Old Testament*. Downers Grove, IL: IVP, 1988.

Wright, Christopher J. H. *The Mission of God: Unlocking the Bible's Grand Narrative*. Downers Grove, IL: IVP Academic, 2006.

Wright, N. T. *Scripture and the Authority of God: How to Read the Bible Today*. New York: HarperOne, 2013.

Wright, N. T. *The New Testament and the People of God*. Minneapolis: Fortress Press, 1992.

Canon and Text of Scripture

Beckwith, Roger T. *The Old Testament Canon of the New Testament Church*. Grand Rapids: Eerdmans, 1986.

Bruce, F. F. *The Canon of Scripture*. Downers Grove, IL: IVP, 1988.

McDonald, Lee Martin. *The Biblical Canon: Its Origin, Transmission, and Authority*. 3rd ed. Peabody, MA: Hendrickson, 2007.

McDonald, Lee Martin, and James A. Sanders, eds. *The Canon Debate*. Peabody, MA: Hendrickson, 2002.

Metzger, Bruce M. *The Canon of the New Testament: Its Origin, Development, and Significance*. Oxford: Clarendon Press, 1987.

Metzger, Bruce M., and Bart D. Ehrman. *The Text of the New Testament: Its Transmission, Corruption, and Restoration*. 4th ed. New York: Oxford University Press, 2005.

Schniedewind, William M. *How the Bible Became a Book: The Textualization of Ancient Israel*. Cambridge: Cambridge University Press, 2004.

Wall, Robert W., and Eugene E. Lemcio. *The New Testament as Canon: A Reader in Canonical Criticism*. Peabody, MA: Hendrickson, 1992.

Translation, Word Studies, and Hermeneutics

Carson, D. A. *Exegetical Fallacies*. 2nd ed. Grand Rapids: Baker, 1996.

Fee, Gordon D., and Douglas Stuart. *How to Read the Bible for All Its Worth*. 4th ed. Grand Rapids: Zondervan, 2014.

Grant, Robert M., and David Tracy. *A Short History of the Interpretation of the Bible*. 2nd ed. Minneapolis: Fortress Press, 1984.

Klein, William W., Craig L. Blomberg, and Robert L. Hubbard Jr. *Introduction to Biblical Interpretation*. 3rd ed. Grand Rapids: Zondervan, 2017.

Porter, Stanley E., and Andrew W. Pitts, eds. *Fundamentals of New Testament Textual Criticism*. Grand Rapids: Eerdmans, 2015.

Ryken, Leland. *The Word of God in English: Criteria for Excellence in Bible Translation*. Wheaton, IL: Crossway, 2002.

Silva, Moisés. *Biblical Words and Their Meaning: An Introduction to Lexical Semantics*. Rev. ed. Grand Rapids: Zondervan, 1994.

Thiselton, Anthony C. *New Horizons in Hermeneutics*. Grand Rapids: Zondervan, 1992.

Wadell, Paul J. *The Primacy of Love: An Introduction to the Ethics of Thomas Aquinas*. Mahwah, NJ: Paulist Press, 1992. (For the link between interpretation and love.)

Old Testament Theology and Key Terms

Brueggemann, Walter. *Theology of the Old Testament: Testimony, Dispute, Advocacy*. Minneapolis: Fortress Press, 1997.

Goldingay, John. *Old Testament Theology*. 3 vols. Downers Grove, IL: IVP Academic, 2003–2009.

Kaiser, Walter C., Jr. *Toward an Old Testament Theology*. Grand Rapids: Zondervan, 1978.

Rad, Gerhard von. *Old Testament Theology*. 2 vols. New York: Harper & Row, 1962–1965.

Waltke, Bruce K., with Charles Yu. *An Old Testament Theology: An Exegetical, Canonical, and Thematic Approach*. Grand Rapids: Zondervan, 2007.

Wenham, Gordon J. *Story as Torah: Reading Old Testament Narrative Ethically*. Edinburgh: T&T Clark, 2000.

Wenham, Gordon J. *The Psalms as Torah: Reading Biblical Song Ethically*. Grand Rapids: Baker Academic, 2012.

Wright, Christopher J. H. *Old Testament Ethics for the People of God*. Downers Grove, IL: IVP, 2004.

New Testament Theology and Use of the Old Testament

Beale, G. K. *A New Testament Biblical Theology: The Unfolding of the Old Testament in the New*. Grand Rapids: Baker Academic, 2011.

Beale, G. K., and D. A. Carson, eds. *Commentary on the New Testament Use of the Old Testament*. Grand Rapids: Baker Academic, 2007.

Marshall, I. Howard. *New Testament Theology: Many Witnesses, One Gospel*. Downers Grove, IL: IVP Academic, 2004.

Moo, Douglas J. *A Theology of Paul and His Letters*. Grand Rapids: Zondervan Academic, 2021.

Schreiner, Thomas R. *New Testament Theology: Magnifying God in Christ.* Grand Rapids: Baker Academic, 2008.

Wright, N. T. *Paul and the Faithfulness of God*. Minneapolis: Fortress Press, 2013.

Lexicons, Dictionaries, and Word-Study Reference Works

Balz, Horst, and Gerhard Schneider, eds. *Exegetical Dictionary of the New Testament*. 3 vols. Grand Rapids: Eerdmans, 1990–1993.

Botterweck, G. Johannes, Helmer Ringgren, and Heinz-Josef Fabry, eds. *Theological Dictionary of the Old Testament*. 15 vols. Grand Rapids: Eerdmans, 1974–2015.

Brown, Colin, ed. *New International Dictionary of New Testament Theology and Exegesis*. Rev. ed. 5 vols. Grand Rapids: Zondervan, 2014.

Freedman, David Noel, ed. *The Anchor Bible Dictionary*. 6 vols. New York: Doubleday, 1992.

Jenni, Ernst, and Claus Westermann, eds. *Theological Lexicon of the Old Testament*. 3 vols. Peabody, MA: Hendrickson, 1997.

Kittel, Gerhard, and Gerhard Friedrich, eds. *Theological Dictionary of the New Testament*. 10 vols. Grand Rapids: Eerdmans, 1964–1976.

Köhler, Ludwig, Walter Baumgartner, and Johann J. Stamm. *The Hebrew and Aramaic Lexicon of the Old Testament*. 2 vols. Leiden: Brill, 1994–2000.

Louw, Johannes P., and Eugene A. Nida. *Greek-English Lexicon of the New Testament Based on Semantic Domains*. 2 vols. New York: United Bible Societies, 1989.

Mounce, William D. *Mounce's Complete Expository Dictionary of Old and New Testament Words*. Grand Rapids: Zondervan, 2006.

Spicq, Ceslas. *Theological Lexicon of the New Testament*. 3 vols. Peabody, MA: Hendrickson, 1994.

VanGemeren, Willem A., ed. *New International Dictionary of Old Testament Theology and Exegesis*. 5 vols. Grand Rapids: Zondervan, 1997.

Studies on Key Themes in This Book

Allison, Dale C. *Jesus and the Victory of God*. Minneapolis: Fortress Press, 1996. (For kingdom, judgment, Gehenna.)

Bauckham, Richard. *Jesus and the God of Israel: God Crucified and Other Studies on the New Testament's Christology of Divine Identity*. Grand Rapids: Eerdmans, 2008. (For YHWH/kyrios and Jesus.)

Brueggemann, Walter. *Peace*. St. Louis: Chalice Press, 2001. (For shalom.)

Brown, Raymond E. *The Death of the Messiah*. 2 vols. New Haven: Yale University Press, 1994. (For covenant, judgment, and salvation in the passion narratives.)

Carson, D. A. *Divine Sovereignty and Human Responsibility*. Eugene, OR: Wipf & Stock, 2002. (For judgment, grace, faith.)

Eichrodt, Walther. *Theology of the Old Testament*. 2 vols. Philadelphia: Westminster Press, 1961–1967. (For covenant and law.)

Marshall, I. Howard. *Aspects of the Atonement: Cross and Resurrection in the Reconciling of God and Humanity*. London: Paternoster, 2007.

Schnackenburg, Rudolf. *The Gospel according to St John*. 3 vols. New York:

Crossroad, 1982. (For Logos, Son of God, and judgment.)

Seifrid, Mark A. *Christ, Our Righteousness: Paul's Theology of Justification*. Downers Grove, IL: IVP, 2000.

Talbert, Charles H. *Reading Luke: A Literary and Theological Commentary*. New York: Crossroad, 1982. (For kingdom, salvation, nations.)

Wright, Christopher J. H. *The Mission of God's People: A Biblical Theology of the Church's Mission*. Grand Rapids: Zondervan, 2010. (For nations/ethnē and covenant.)

Wright, N. T. *Surprised by Hope: Rethinking Heaven, the Resurrection, and the Mission of the Church*. New York: HarperOne, 2008. (For resurrection, judgment, and new creation.)

Study Bibles and Digital Tools

The ESV Study Bible. Wheaton, IL: Crossway, 2008.

The NIV Study Bible. Fully Revised Edition. Grand Rapids: Zondervan, 2020.

The NRSV Cultural Backgrounds Study Bible. Grand Rapids: Zondervan, 2019.

Logos Bible Software. Faithlife Corporation. Accordance Bible Software. OakTree Software. Olive Tree Bible App. Harper Collins Christian Publishing. YouVersion Bible App. Life. Church.

References

These sources are written for serious study, but even a quick look at their main conclusions can deepen the simple points this chapter has tried to make clear.

Chapter 4

- Studies on Exodus 3:14 and the divine name

- D. A. Carson, "Exodus 3:14: God's Self-Revelation," in various commentaries on Exodus.

- Eberhard Jüngel, discussions of Exodus 3:14 and the name of God in modern theology.

- A. H. Ehrman, "Ehyeh Asher Ehyeh (Exodus 3:14): God's 'Narrative Identity' Among Moses and Israel," *Poetics Today* 31 (2010).

- Scholarly articles on "Ehyeh asher ehyeh" that argue for relational and narrative readings of the name.

- Studies on YHWH, the Tetragrammaton, and Jewish practice

- "Tetragrammaton," *Jewish Encyclopedia* (historical survey of the name and its avoidance).

- Discussions of the Tetragrammaton and its pronunciation in standard Old Testament introductions and theologies.

- Articles on the development of reverence for the name and the substitution of "Adonai."

- Studies on YHWH and Kyrios in the Septuagint

- H. B. Swete, *An Introduction to the Old Testament in Greek* (classic work on the Greek OT).

- Articles on the use of **Kyrios** as a substitute for the Tetragrammaton in the Septuagint and on whether it functions as a name in those contexts.

- Larry W. Hurtado, blog essays and scholarly articles on the divine name and early Christian devotion.

- Studies on "Kyrios" and "ego eimi" in the New Testament

- Richard Bauckham, *Jesus and the God of Israel* (on how New Testament writers include Jesus in the identity of the God of Israel).

- Raymond E. Brown, *The Gospel According to John* (detailed commentary, including on the "I am" sayings).

- Academic articles on the "ego eimi" sayings in John and their possible connections to Exodus 3 and to "I am" statements in Isaiah in the Greek Old Testament.

Chapter 5

On Elohim in the Hebrew Bible

- Standard Old Testament introductions and theologies that discuss *'elohim* as a plural form used with singular verbs for Israel's God.

- Articles that examine the singular/plural behavior of *'elohim* and its use for both the true God and for other gods.

- Studies of Israelite monotheism and the "divine council" that explore how *'elohim* can refer to various spiritual beings while maintaining the uniqueness of YHWH.

On Adonai and the substitution for the divine name

- Reference works on the Tetragrammaton and Jewish reading traditions that explain the practice of saying "Adonai" instead of pronouncing YHWH.

- Discussions of the distinction between *'adon*, *'adoni*, and *'adonai* in Hebrew and how these are rendered in translations.

On Kyrios in the Septuagint and New Testament

- Studies of the Septuagint that trace how **Kyrios** is used to represent YHWH and Adonai in the Greek Old Testament.

- Larry W. Hurtado and others on the use of Kyrios as a reverential substitute for the divine name and its implications for early Christian worship.

- Academic work on Kyrios in the New Testament, exploring how the same word is used for God, for Jesus, and for human lords, and how Old Testament YHWH texts are applied to Christ.

Chapter 6

On the names Yehoshua, Yeshua, and their meanings

- Standard Hebrew name dictionaries and lexicons that derive **Yehoshua** from elements meaning "YHWH" and "salvation," yielding "YHWH is salvation / saves."

- Studies on the shortening of theophoric names (names containing "Yeho-" or "Yo-") and the development of the shorter form **Yeshua** in late biblical Hebrew and Aramaic.

- Articles and monographs that discuss the occurrence of the name Yeshua in books like Ezra and Nehemiah and in inscriptions.

On the Greek form Iēsous and the link between Joshua and Jesus

- Septuagint studies showing that **Joshua son of Nun** is called **Iēsous** in the Greek Old Testament, and that the same Greek form is used for **Jesus of Nazareth** in the New Testament.

- Works on New Testament onomastics (the study of names) that trace the path: Yehoshua → Yeshua → Iēsous → Jesus.

- Scholarly discussions of Hebrews and other New Testament writings that explore the typological connection between Joshua and Jesus.

On Matthew 1:21 and the theology of Jesus' name

- Academic commentaries on Matthew that highlight the word-play in 1:21 ("you shall call his name Jesus, for he will save his people from their sins") and discuss how the name's meaning supports Matthew's portrait of Jesus as the one through whom God saves His people.

- Articles focusing specifically on Matthew 1:21 that examine how the verse links Jesus' identity, His name, and His saving mission.

Chapter 7

On mashiach ("anointed one") in the Old Testament

- Standard Hebrew lexicons and theological wordbooks that define **māshîach** as "anointed one" and survey its use for kings, priests, and others.

- Studies of anointing rituals in the Old Testament, including the anointing of Saul, David, and the high priest, and the symbolic link between oil and the Spirit.

- Discussions of Isaiah's use of "anointed" language, including the surprising application of the term to Cyrus.

On christos in the Septuagint and New Testament

- Works on the Septuagint that trace how **christos** is used to translate **mashiach** in the Greek Old Testament.

- New Testament word studies that explain how **christos** functions first as a title ("the Christ") and later also as a name closely attached to Jesus.

- Studies of early Christian confessions (like Peter's, and the opening of Mark and Matthew) that explore how "Christ" is used to identify Jesus as the expected Messiah.

On messianic expectations in Second Temple Judaism

- Surveys of Jewish messianic expectations in the Second Temple period, showing the variety of royal, priestly, prophetic, and sometimes heavenly Messiah figures in different texts.

- Academic discussions of how Jesus both fits and reshapes those expectations in the New Testament.

On Christ as Prophet, Priest, and King

- Classic and modern theological works that present Christ's three-fold office and connect it to Old Testament anointing of prophets, priests, and kings.

- Bible studies that explore how the New Testament presents Jesus as fulfilling these roles (especially in the Gospels and in Hebrews).

Chapter 8

On "sons of God" in the Old Testament

- Studies of the phrase "sons of God" in Job, Psalms, and Genesis, examining its use for heavenly beings and members of God's council.

- Scholarly articles on Israel as God's "firstborn son" in Exodus and the implications for covenant theology.

- Work on royal ideology in Israel that explores 2 Samuel 7 and Psalm 2 and the "adoption" of the king as God's son.

On Second Temple Jewish uses of "son of God"

- Surveys of Jewish texts between the Testaments that discuss messianic hopes and "son of God" language for future royal or heavenly figures.

- Studies comparing "son of God" and "son of man" expectations in Second Temple Judaism.

On "Son of God" as a title for Jesus

- Academic work on the Synoptic Gospels (Matthew, Mark, Luke) that defines "Son of God" as a royal, messianic title rooted in Old Testament promises, and also as expressing Jesus' unique relationship with God.

- Studies that trace how the Gospels present Jesus as Son in ways that link Him to David, Israel, and Adam, while also presenting Him as sharing in God's identity.

- Theological essays that explore how Jesus' unique sonship relates to believers' adopted sonship in the New Testament.

Chapter 9

On "son of man" in the Old Testament and Second Temple Judaism

- Studies of the Hebrew phrase *ben 'adam* in Psalms, Ezekiel, and other texts, showing its use as an idiom for "human being" and for emphasizing human frailty.

- Scholarly work on Daniel 7 that examines the "one like a son of man" as a human-like figure who receives authority and a kingdom from the Ancient of Days, and explores whether he represents Israel, an individual, or both.

- Surveys of Second Temple Jewish literature (including apocalyptic writings) that trace how Daniel's "son of man" imagery was developed into expectations about an exalted, end-time figure.

On "Son of Man" as Jesus' self-title

- Academic studies of the "Son of Man" sayings in the Gospels that categorize them into present-mission, suffering, and future-glory sayings, and discuss how Jesus uses the title in each group.

- Essays that argue that "Son of Man" was not a fixed, widely recognized title before Jesus, but that He filled it with meaning drawn from Scripture, especially Daniel 7.

- Works that explore how the early church understood "Son of Man" in relation to Jesus' humanity, His exaltation, and His role as judge.

On theology of "Son of Man" today

- Theological reflections that show how "Son of Man" complements "Son of God": one emphasizing Christ's true humanity and His representative role, the other emphasizing His unique relationship to the Father.

- Bible-study resources that walk readers through all the "Son of Man" references in a particular Gospel to see the title in action.

Chapter 10

On "word of the LORD" and Logos

- Old Testament studies on the phrase "the word of the LORD," showing how it functions as God's active, effective speech in creation and prophecy.

- Septuagint research tracing how Hebrew *dābār* is translated with **logos** and how "word" language is used for divine action.

- New Testament word studies on **logos** that distinguish its ordinary uses ("word, message") from its unique use in John 1, 1 John 1:1, and Revelation 19:13.

On Wisdom in Proverbs, Sirach, and Wisdom of Solomon

- Commentaries and articles on Proverbs 8 and related passages that treat Wisdom as a personification of God's wise, creative work rather than a separate deity.

- Studies of Wisdom in Sirach and Wisdom of Solomon that explore Wisdom's pre-existence, connection to Torah, and role in God's dealings with Israel.

- Scholarly discussions of "Wisdom Christology," exploring how New Testament writers may allude to Wisdom traditions when speaking about Christ.

On Immanuel in Isaiah and Matthew

- Academic work on Isaiah 7–8 that situates the Immanuel prophecy in the historical crisis of King Ahaz and explains how the name functions as a sign of "God with us."

- Studies of Matthew's use of Isaiah 7:14 in Matthew 1:23, examining how he sees Jesus as the deeper fulfillment of the Immanuel promise.

On Logos theology in John

- Commentaries and essays on John 1:1–18 that discuss Jewish Scriptural background (Word and Wisdom) and Greek philosophical background for the term **Logos**.

- Theological treatments of "Logos theology" that explain how the early church understood Jesus as God's Word made flesh, uniting God's transcendence and presence.

Chapter 11

On nephesh in the Old Testament

- Hebrew lexicons and theological wordbooks that define **nephesh** as "living being, life, self, person, appetite, inner being," and survey its uses across narrative, law, and poetry.

- Studies and word-study videos that emphasize that nephesh is not a disembodied soul but a breathing creature, and that humans **are** nephesh rather than simply "having" one.

- Articles that trace how nephesh can refer to animals, humans, inner experience, and even a dead body, stressing context-dependent meaning.

On psychē in the New Testament

- Greek lexicons that define **psychē** as "life, self, inner life, soul" and note its frequent use in the Septuagint to translate nephesh.

- New Testament word studies that examine psychē in Jesus' sayings and in letters, showing where it is best translated "life" and where "soul" captures the emphasis on inner or ongoing personal existence.

- Scholarly discussions of how the New Testament balances the broad

Hebrew sense of psychē (as whole person and life) with later distinctions between soul, spirit, and body.

On the nephesh–psychē connection

- Comparative studies of Old Testament nephesh passages and their Greek versions using psychē, including texts later quoted in the New Testament (such as Psalm 16:10 and Acts 2:27).

- Essays warning against reading later philosophical notions of an immortal, separable soul back into biblical terms that originally focused on the whole living person.

Chapter 12

You can move these into a consolidated reference section at the back of the book; they are grouped here by topic.

On ruach in the Old Testament

- Hebrew lexicons and theological wordbooks that define **ruach** as "wind, breath, spirit" and survey its uses for natural wind, human breath, human spirit, and God's Spirit.

- Studies tracing ruach in key passages like Genesis 1:2, Ezekiel 37, and the narratives of judges and kings where God's Spirit comes upon people.

- Articles exploring how ancient Israelites understood the connection between breath, life, and spirit.

On pneuma in the New Testament

- Greek lexicons that define **pneuma** as "wind, breath, spirit" and catalogue its uses for the Holy Spirit, human spirits, angels, demons, and natural wind.

- Word studies on pneuma in John 3, Romans 8, and 1 Corinthians, highlighting the link between the Spirit and new life, guidance, and power.

- Surveys of New Testament teaching on the Holy Spirit that emphasize both His personal nature and the ongoing use of wind/breath imagery.

On the ruach–pneuma connection

- Comparative studies of ruach in the Hebrew Bible and pneuma in the Greek Old Testament and New Testament, showing continuity in imagery and meaning.

- Essays on early Christian "pneumatology" (teaching about the Spirit) that start from the broad semantic range of ruach and pneuma and warn against flattening "Spirit" into either a mere force or a vague feeling.

Chapter 13

You can move these into a consolidated reference section at the back of the book; they are grouped here by topic.

On basar in the Old Testament

- Hebrew lexicons and theological wordbooks that define **bāśār** as "flesh, body, person, kin, mankind" and discuss its use for physical tissue, family relationship, and "all flesh" as humanity in its frailty.

- Studies of basar in covenant and prophetic contexts, especially phrases like "we are your bone and flesh" and "all flesh shall see."

On sarx and sōma in the New Testament

- Greek lexicons that define **sarx** as "flesh" in literal and metaphorical senses (soft tissue, humanity, human nature under sin) and **sōma** as "body" (physical body, whole person, corporate body).

- Detailed word studies of sarx in Paul's letters, highlighting the difference between neutral uses (flesh/body) and negative uses (flesh as the realm of sin).

- Studies of sōma that explore its role in teaching on resurrection, the Lord's Supper, and the church as the body of Christ.

On body, flesh, and Christian theology

- Theological works that address the biblical view of the body, resisting dualism and emphasizing embodied existence, resurrection hope, and the body as temple of the Spirit.

- Bible-study resources that trace "flesh vs Spirit" themes in Romans and Galatians and show how they describe competing ways of life rather than a simple body-vs-soul split.

Chapter 14

You can move these into a consolidated reference section at the back of the book; they are grouped here by topic.

On lev / levav in the Old Testament

- Hebrew word studies and lexicons that define **lev / levav** as the center of thought, will, emotion, and moral life, and note its role in Deuteronomy 6:5 and many psalms.facebook+5

- Studies of the "heart" in Proverbs and prophetic literature, especially on guarding the heart and God's promise to give a new heart.

On kardia in the New Testament

- Greek lexicons and word studies that describe **kardia** as the figurative heart: the inner person, including intellect, emotion, desire, and will.

- Articles tracing kardia through the Gospels and letters, showing how it functions as the place of faith, understanding, and moral decision.

On the biblical concept of the heart as unified inner center

- Comparative studies showing continuity between Hebrew **lev** and Greek **kardia** and emphasizing that the biblical "heart" unites what we often separate into "mind" and "feelings."

- Theological reflections on "new heart" language in Jeremiah, Ezekiel, and the New Testament, highlighting God's work of inner transformation rather than mere emotional change.

Suggested Sources for Further Study (Chapter 15)

You can move these into a consolidated reference section at the back of the book; they are grouped here by topic.

On Sheol in the Hebrew Bible

- Articles and monographs that define **Sheol** as the underworld realm of the dead, linked with "grave" and "pit," and survey its uses across the Old Testament.

- Studies that distinguish Sheol from later, more developed concepts of hell, and explore texts that express hope in God's power to rescue from Sheol.

On Hades in the New Testament and Greek background

- Bible dictionaries and encyclopedias that explain **Hades** as the Greek counterpart to Sheol, the realm of the dead, and discuss its appearances in the New Testament, including Acts 2 and Luke 16.

- Works that trace how Hades functions both as a general term for the state of the dead and, in some passages, as a place of conscious torment for the wicked awaiting final judgment.

On Gehenna and the Valley of Hinnom

- Historical and geographical studies of the **Valley of Hinnom** near Jerusalem, its association with idolatry and child sacrifice, and later images of burning refuse.

- Research on **Gehenna** as a Jewish term for judgment, showing how Jesus' use of the word draws on this local, historical imagery rather than introducing a brand-new idea.

On Tartarus and angelic judgment

- Commentaries on 2 Peter that discuss **Tartarus** in 2 Peter 2:4, its Greek mythological background, and its use to describe a prison for rebellious angels awaiting judgment.

____

About the author

Rene' Stanley is a veteran, storyteller, and Bible teacher who loves to put real life and real faith on the same page. Born and raised amid the historic streets of Washington, D.C., and later shaped by her service in the U.S. Army during Desert Storm, she writes with the steady realism of someone who has seen both hardship and grace up close.booksbyrene+1

Over the course of more than thirty books, Rene' has explored hope, loss, and transformation in urban coming-of-age stories like *Sheltered in the Storm: A Tale of Respect and Redemption, Shadows and Light: The Journey of Jasmin and Marcus, Roots of Faith,* and *Leaving the Game: A Tale of Transformation.* She has also written practical, church-facing works such as *Heaven's Blueprint: Trusting God's Plan for You* and *The Ministry of Giving Laughter, Lessons, and Love,* along with devotional resources and guides for young believers, parents, and those navigating grief and change.everand+5

What Did It Say First? Hearing the Bible in Its Own Words grows out of that same calling: to make deep things understandable, and to help ordinary Christians hear Scripture more clearly without needing formal training. Drawing on her love of story, her experience listening across generations, and her own journey through diverse church traditions, Rene' invites readers into a calmer, wiser way of reading the Bible—one that honors both the ancient words and the people who are trying to live by them today.

Readers can discover more about Rene's work at www.books-by-rene.store